Super Reader

HOW TO TEACH YOUR CHILD TO SPEED READ

Super Reader

Bonnie Bauman

Illustrated by Abby Crisses

A SCARBOROUGH BOOK

Thanks to Grosset & Dunlap for the use of excerpts from their
Junior Illustrated Library.

First published in 1979
Copyright © 1979 by Bonnie Bauman
Super Reader Song, music and lyrics copyright © 1978 by Jonathan L. Segal
All rights reserved
Printed in the United States of America
Stein and Day/Publishers/Scarborough House
Briarcliff Manor, N.Y. 10510

Library of Congress Cataloging in Publication Data

Bauman, Bonnie.
  Super reader.

  1. Rapid reading.   I. Crisses, Abby.   II. Title.
LB1050.54.B38   372.4'14   76-56192
ISBN 0-8128-2454-7
    0-8128-2453-9 pbk.

To the first Super Reader—
my son KIDON,
who assisted,
encouraged, and
most of all
inspired me

Contents

INTRODUCTION FOR
PARENTS AND TEACHERS

Super Reader is designed to make silent reading an easy, happy, and fun-filled experience for children of elementary-school age. Parents and teachers know that if children can do something well, they will enjoy doing it. Most children do not enjoy reading to themselves because they can't do it well. Perhaps they were never taught how to read silently. The emphasis in the schoolroom has often been on teaching children basic oral reading skills. Once this is accomplished, the children are frequently left to their own devices. Years later, as adults, they find that their reading skills are often unequal to the reading requirements of their jobs or of their leisure reading appetites. The proliferation of speed-reading books and speed-reading courses points up the crisis in adult reading and comprehension.

To grasp this problem, let's begin with an understanding of how our children are taught to read in school. Today there are many methods and combinations of methods, but the most common are the *phonic* method and the *look-say* method. In both processes, the child has been taught to read by saying the words, or *vocalizing*. After the child has accomplished this, he is told to read to himself and is then left alone.

But a child should not read to himself the same way he reads aloud. This is where the *Super Reader* methods come into play. The methods are composites of established speed-reading techniques which have proven successful for adults.* The techniques have been altered and simplified for use by children. Though the techniques are similar to speed-reading techniques, *speed is not a primary concern in and of itself.* The *quality* achieved in reading, rather than the quantity, is stressed throughout. After all, speed-reading is just silent reading done the right way.

This book is written for every parent or teacher who wants to teach their children or students how to truly read silently, and therefore more effectively. It will explain how to teach children to read without moving their lips or throat muscles, and show how to teach them to avoid saying the words to themselves as they read. Most important, it will demonstrate how to teach your children to read in

---

* Of course your child could learn to speed read at twenty, but then it is so much harder to break a ten-year habit of reading one word at a time. If your child learns *now* you will be able to avoid many of the problems that seem to occur in later years.

groups of words instead of reading one word at a time. Each of the techniques is offered as a means of making reading easier and more fun.

It should be emphasized that a sense of humor is vital to this undertaking. Your child will do better and accomplish more if she's having a good time. Make her laugh. Help her to enjoy herself and have fun. Hopefully, this book will offer many opportunities for a wonderful experience, one for just the two of you to share. You must be relaxed and without tension. Your young reader must not be made to fear failure or punishment.

For the elementary schoolteacher, *Super Reader* can be used as a supplement to the required English course.

All the necessary tools and materials are provided in the book, but *you* must must give them life and spirit. It takes about three to six months to master all the skills. Fifteen to twenty minutes three times a week is all that is needed. If you realize that it took several years for your child to learn how to read aloud, then the time spent in teaching how to read silently shouldn't seem long. During this time it will be your job to keep your child enthusiastic about the project. You must provide inspiration. Praise, flatter, and applaud. Anything that takes time obviously requires patience. If you have patience, your child will have patience, too.

Be sure that you don't isolate your child's reading skill. This skill is a means to an end, not an end in itself. Let your child know that nearly everything he wants to know can be found in books. If your child is interested in baseball, he can read about the rules of the game, the origins of the game, and the lives of great baseball players. If he or she is interested in horses, dancing, butterflies, collecting stamps, astronomy, or any other possible subject, remind the child that one can read more and thus learn more about it. Convince your children that the more they know, the more life can be enjoyed. You might also suggest to them that the new reading skills will allow them to do their homework in half the time it now takes, thus leaving more time for other interests and activities.

To achieve progress in reading, your child must be consistent. You can lead your child in this direction by encouraging him to stick to a predetermined schedule. You can help set up a schedule—it should be a relaxed and easy one—and adhere to it. At the beginning you might want to spend one or two nights a week with your child.

Before you begin the *Super Reader* program, look through the entire book to get an overall feeling for the material, the way it is organized and what it hopes to accomplish. Be sure to go over each chapter carefully before you introduce it to your pupil. The directions and explanations are written for you; the exercises are for your child.

The Super Reader character was created as a guide for your child. He offers advice, directions, and fun throughout the book. At the conclusion of the first three chapters there is a special review section called "Super Reader Says." By going over these sections carefully, you will be able to measure your child's progress. Proceed to the next chapter only if he or she can do all the exercises on these pages. Badges are provided at each level. Have your child *trace,* color, and cut and paste them on a T-shirt.

The structure of the book relates to the known obstacles to effective silent reading and the means to overcome these. The major obstacles are:

1. Reading too slowly.
2. Regression (habitually looking back).
3. Reading word by word.
4. Saying the words to oneself while reading.
5. Weak vocabulary.
6. Poor comprehension.

In Chapter 1, the moving finger forces the eyes to move faster. Why faster? If a child reads slowly, he understands *less,* not more. Reading faster will eliminate fatigue, prevent boredom, and block distractions. As the child's reading speed increases, so will his comprehension.

In Chapter 2, solutions are offered to the problem of reading word by word. Your child is shown how to widen his visual span by using peripheral vision. In this way your child learns how to read in groups of words or thought-units.

Chapter 3 deals with the universally common problem of vocalizing (saying the words in your throat, or moving your lips) and subvocalizing (hearing the words in your mind as you read). These can be partially eliminated by reading faster, by reading in groups of words, and by saying something else aloud to inhibit saying the words you are reading in your mind.

Chapter 4, the Super Reader Olympics, offers your child wonderful clues to improve speed and comprehension.

Without a knowledge of words, how can you read? In the final chapter, your children are encouraged to become word collectors to further increase their vocabulary and thus widen their reading skills.

Super Reader's Introduction

Hi!

I'm Super Reader and I'm here to help you learn how to

  speed-read.

This book isn't all work. We're going to have plenty of fun—

  with snakes and stones,

  trains and exercises,

  eyeglasses and tricks.

  I know you'll like speed-reading because it will make reading much *easier!* You'll be able to read many more books, your grades will improve in school, and you'll have more time for other interests as well.

This book has four chapters of lessons and exercises plus a fifth chapter at the end with some interesting games.

In Chapter 1, believe it or not, you will learn how to read faster by following a snake. Then, as a beginning speed reader, you will be a Rookie Reader and receive a badge.

Chapter 2 takes you for a ride on the Reading Railroad, where you'll learn how to read in groups of words. Then you will become a Rapid Reader.

Pencils, straws, tulips, and tangerines all join forces in Chapter 3 to teach you how to sight-read. You will earn another badge and become an Accelerated Reader.

And finally, what we've all been waiting for—the Super Olympics. Chapter 4 teaches you special ways to increase your reading speed and improve your comprehension. At the Olympics, you must first pass the qualifying warm-ups, then jump the hurdles, and finally run the laps. And when you've done all that, you earn a Gold Medal and become a

Super Reader

Good luck and

Have Fun!

Follow
the
Snake

FOLLOW THE SNAKE

Follow the snake? What snake? And what does following a snake have to do with speed-reading?

Your child was taught to read by reading aloud. After he could read aloud, he was told to read to himself, and that is exactly what happened. He read to himself exactly the same way he read aloud, word by word, only now you couldn't hear him. The end result was a child who could read only as fast as he could talk—and that's not the most efficient way to read. Everyone should read faster than he can talk because *reading fast improves comprehension.*

How is this possible? If a child reads fast, she won't have the time to become bored, tired, or distracted. And if she's not bored, tired, or distracted, her concentration will improve, and her comprehension will soar. The first thing for the child to learn is how to go faster. And that's where the snake comes in.

Instruct your child in his first exercise. Tell him that this is a special assignment. Explain that this first assignment will prepare him to master all the tricks in the book. Assure him that the exercise will be easy. It will start him on the road to reading faster than he normally reads—but emphasize that he must not read so fast that he no longer understands what he has read.

Offer this clue to get her started. Tell her that she has lazy eyes that have to be pushed to go faster. How can that be done? Show her how to follow a snake with her finger. She may use either her middle finger or her index finger, whichever is more comfortable.

Starting at the snake's tail in the top left-hand part of the page, show your child how to let his eyes look slightly above the finger as it follows the snake, swinging across and down at a steady rhythmic pace.

Do the exercise as many times as he needs to.

Follow the Snake

Ready? Here we go.
Place your finger here
and follow the snake
in the direction of
the arrows.

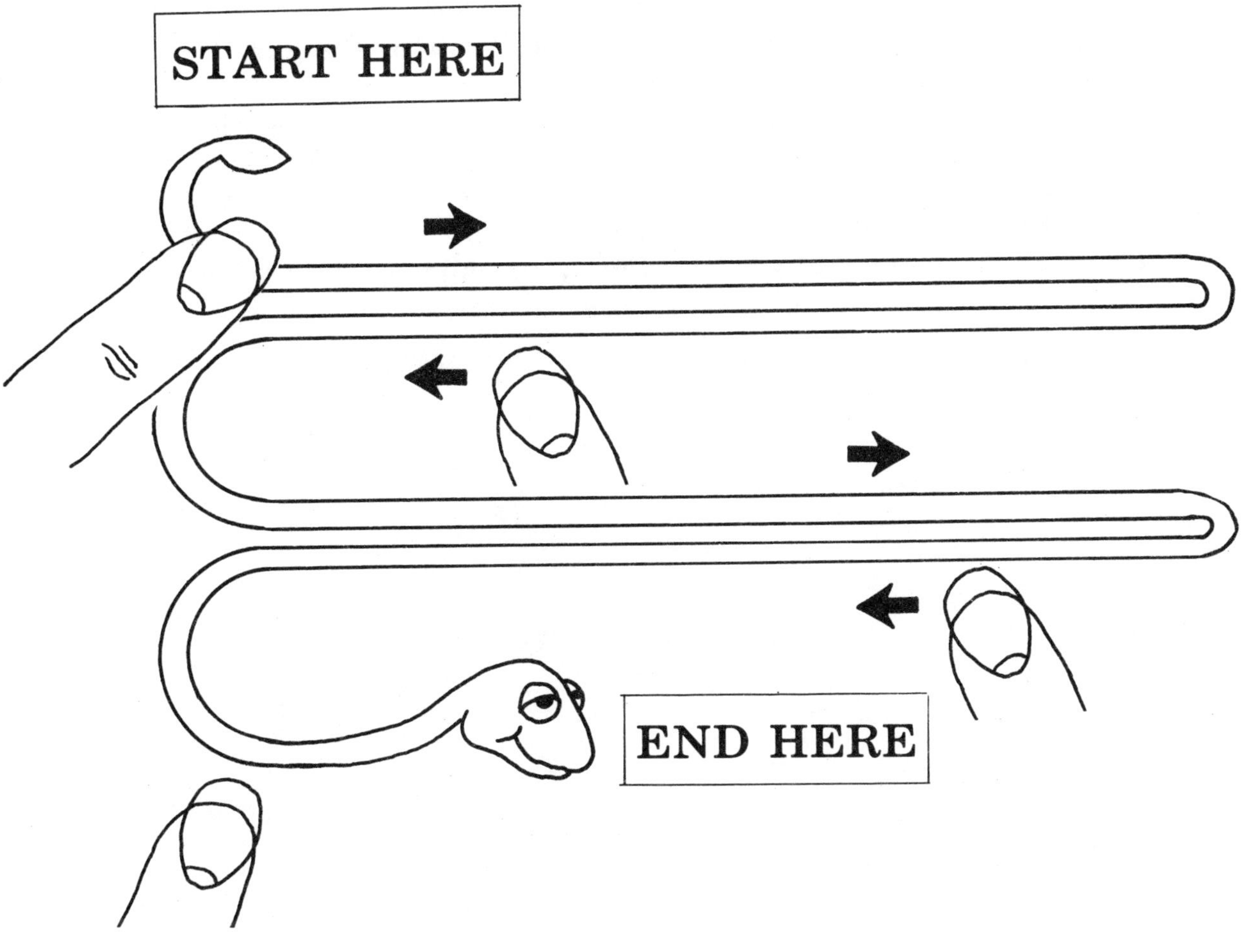

START HERE

END HERE

Now let's add words to the exercise. Have your child *read the sentence* to himself as he follows the snake. You can draw an analogy for your child by comparing the role of his finger to the role of the rabbit in dog races. As the dog chases the rabbit, so do the eyes race along behind the finger.

Don't let your child press down too hard with her finger. She should let her finger touch the page lightly and smoothly. Make sure her eyes are focused slightly above her finger as it follows the snake.

Most important of all, make it a game.

Encourage and praise your child. Remember that it is easy for your child to be a lazy reader. Reading correctly is work at first, so it will be your role to make that work more enjoyable. Be sure that you don't nag. Try to work when your child is refreshed.

Here are five additional selections for your child to practice on. Have fun!

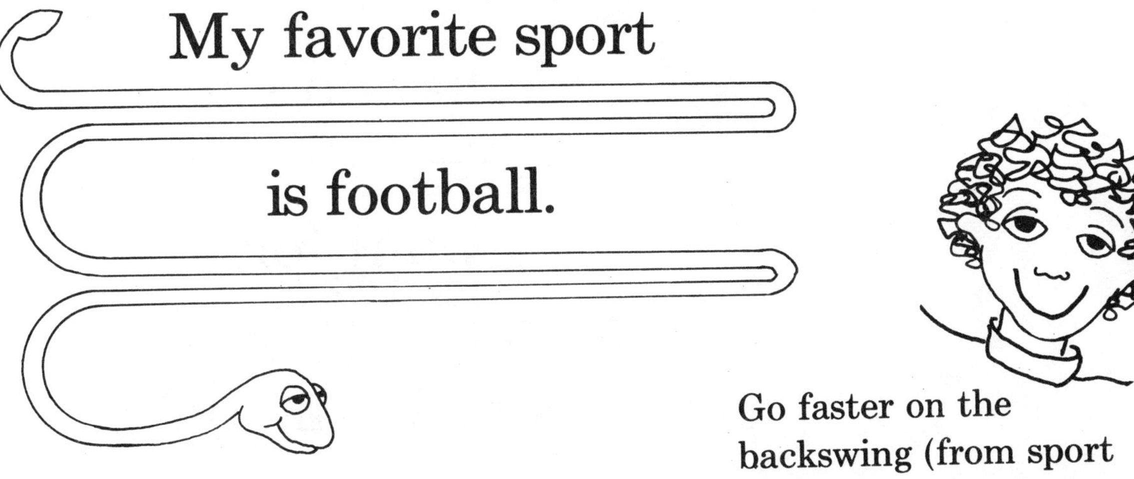

Go faster on the backswing (from sport to is). You can go faster because you're not reading from *sport* to *is*.

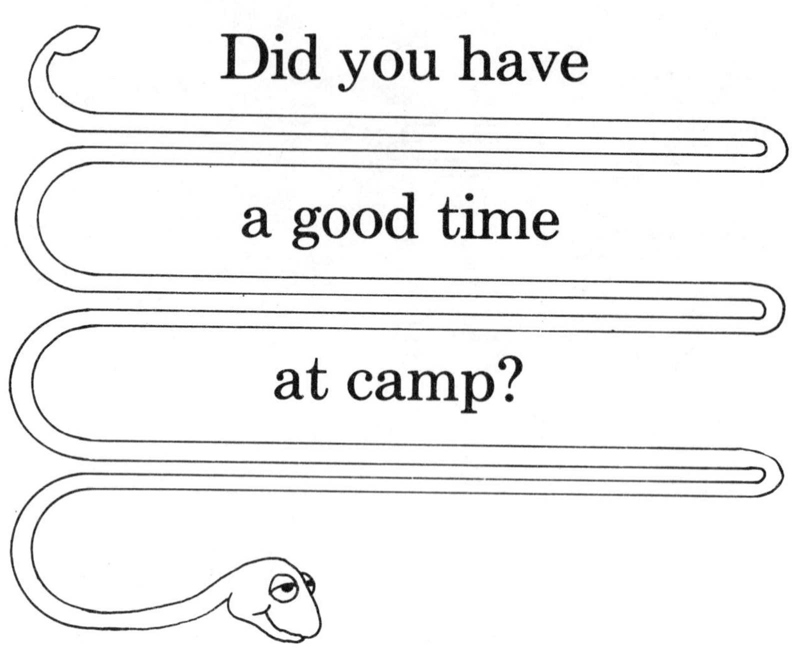

Did you have
a good time
at camp?

What do you
want for
your birthday?

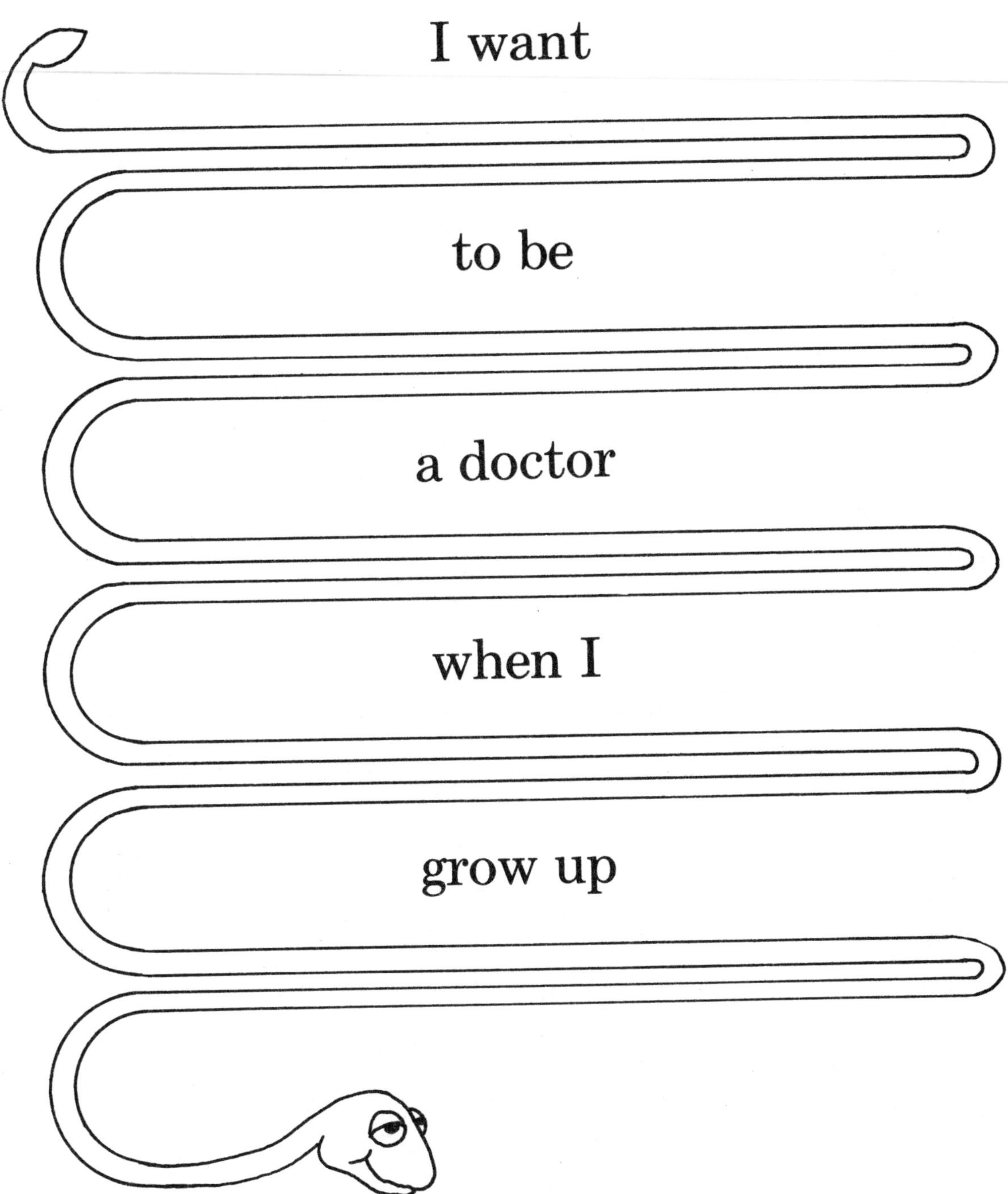

I want
to be
a doctor
when I
grow up

DON'T LOOK BACK

The habit of continuously looking back to see if you missed something is called *regression*. If there is really something that is missed or not understood, then your child should return to it, but most times children who regress do it unconsciously, even if they have understood everything they have read. The steady rhythmic pace of following the snake helps to overcome regression. Once your child is conscious of the regression habit, it will be easy to break.

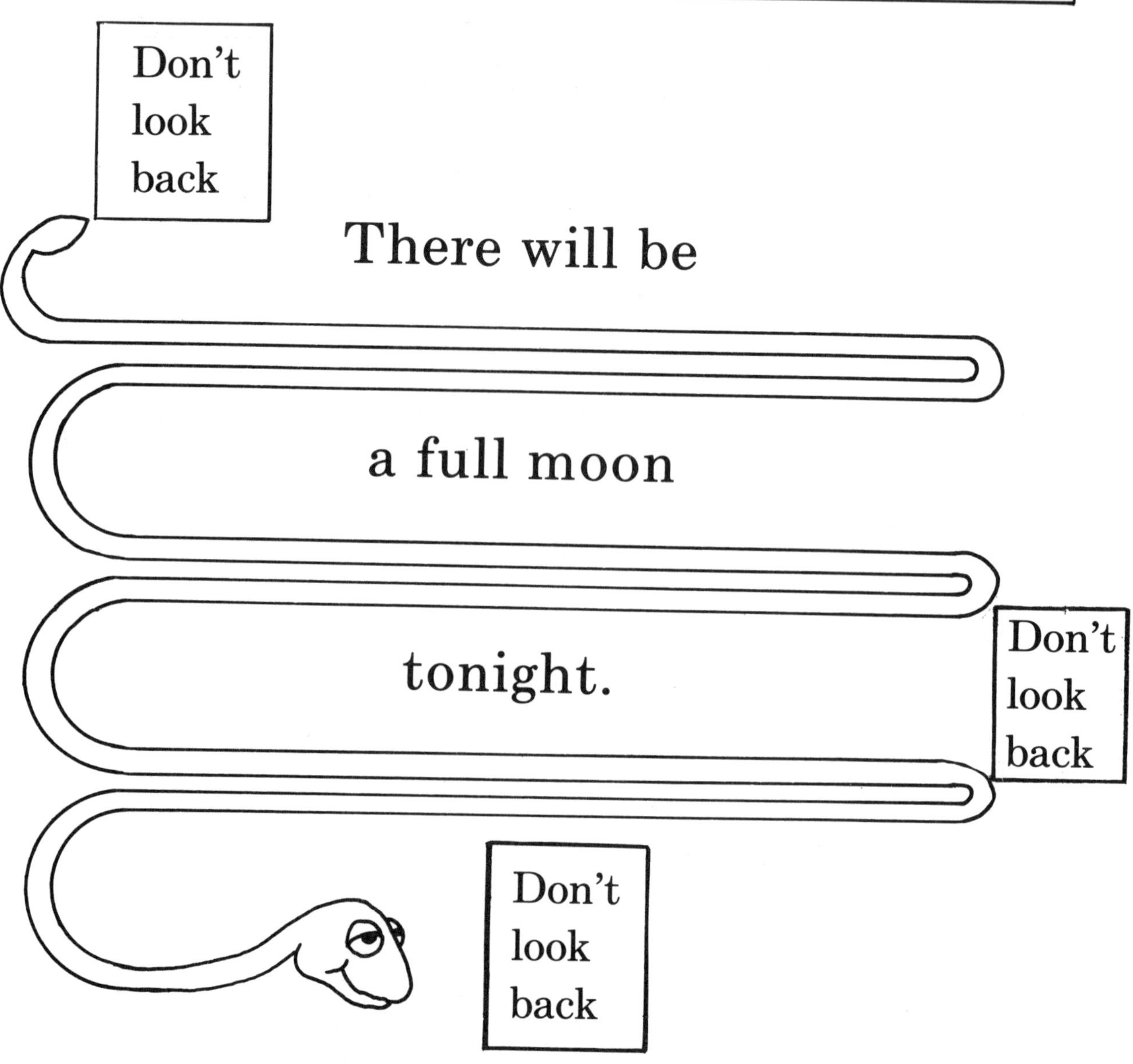

Don't Look Back

However, if you don't
understand something, you
may look back and check
the meaning.
Keep a steady flow,
across and down the page
as you follow the snake.

The house whirled

around a couple of times

and rose slowly

through the air!

From *The Wizard of Oz*
by L. Frank Baum

READ AND RECITE

It's important not to let your child follow the snake so fast that he doesn't know what he's reading. At the beginning, check by asking him to tell you about the selection. If he can't tell you what he has just read, then he's going too fast. Tell him to slow down. After he finds a pace that is faster than his normal pace, but not so fast that he retains little or nothing, you can let him check on his own by reciting to himself what the selection is about. This is called a "Read and Recite."

Here are some practice selections.

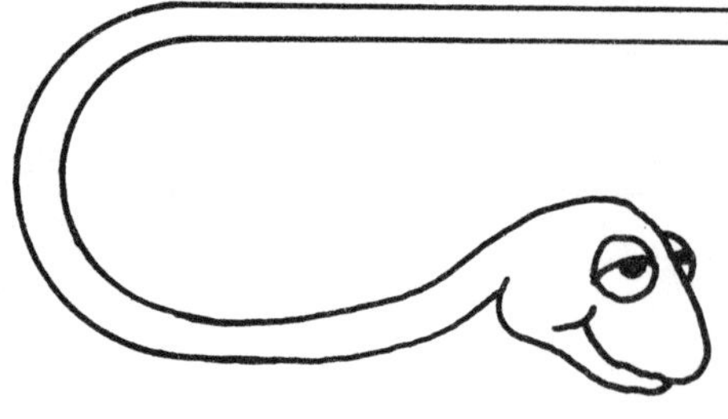

From *Swiss Family Robinson*
by Johann R. Wyss

Read and Recite

Do a Read and Recite
with these selections.

Either the well was very deep,

or she fell very slowly,

for she had plenty of time

as she went down to look about her,

and to wonder what was going to happen next.

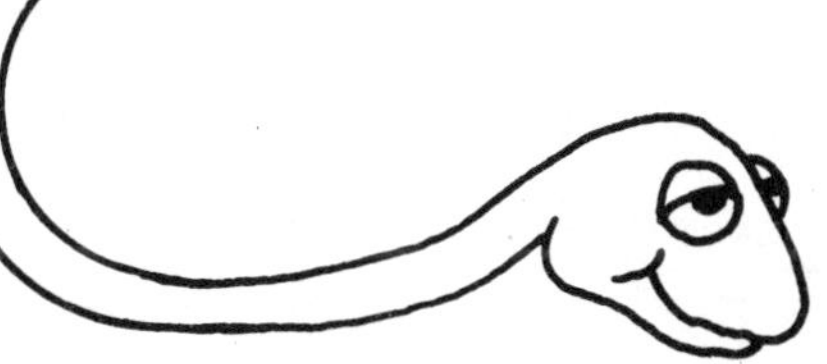

From *Alice in Wonderland*
by Lewis Carroll

OUTSIDE READING

Explain to your child that the snake was drawn only for this book. When she is reading other books, the snake will have to be *imaginary*. Only she will see it and be able to follow it. Persuade your child to choose an *easy* book of fiction, and have her follow the imaginary snake at least fifteen minutes a day for anywhere between two to four weeks. Say, "Perhaps at first that snake will act like a lazy fellow, but after a week or so he should be snazzy, jazzy, and speedy."

Make certain that your children have a schedule to follow. You may want to sit with them one or two nights a week. Review the steps suggested by Super Reader on page 15. Discuss their progress.

Continue to expose your children to a wide selection of books. Take them to the library and bookstores with you. Talk about books. Let them feel confident and comfortable in telling you their reactions to the books they have been reading. After they complete this chapter, congratulate them on becoming a Rookie Reader. Have them trace and color the Rookie Reader badge found on page 28 on a piece of bond paper. Then cut out the badge and pin it on their sweaters or shirts.

Observe your child's success, and when you feel that he is ready and wants to go on, proceed to Chapter 2. "It is now time," you say, "to work toward becoming a Rapid Reader."

Here are a few of my favorite books.

If you like mysteries, try these	*Alfred Hitchcock Presents: Slay Rides* ed. by Alfred Hitchcock, The Hardy Boys books, *The Mystery of the Spiral Bridge* by Franklin W. Dixon.
If you like animals, try these	*The Yearling* by Marjorie Kinnan Rawlings, *Old Yeller* by Frederick Gipson, *A Midnight Fox* by Betsy Byars.
If you like adventures, try these	*The Call of the Wild* by Jack London, *The Incredible Journey* by Sheila Burnford.
If you like fantasy, try these	*Charlotte's Web* by E. B. White, *A Wrinkle in Time* by Madeline L'Engle.
If you like science fiction, try these	*Journey to the Center of the Earth* by Jules Verne, *The Time Machine* by H. G. Wells.
If you like classics, try these	*Black Beauty* by Anna Sewell, *Treasure Island* by Robert Louis Stevenson.
If you like sports, try these	*Baseball Sparkplug* by Matt Christopher, *O. J. Simpson* by Ray Hill.
If you like biographies, try these	*Meet Martin Luther King* by James T. DeKay, *Meet JFK* by Nancy Bean White, *Albert Einstein* by Arthur Beckhard.

Take a Break

Time Out! Give a Shout!

SUPER READER SAYS DO THIS

Choose an easy fiction book and practice *Following the Snake.*

You may want to read two or three nights a week—or more.

Read and Recite

While you are following the snake, be sure that you're not going TOO fast. If you read TOO fast, you won't be able to enjoy your book because you won't understand what you've read. So after you've finished, try to recite aloud some of the highlights of the selection. If you can't think of anything to say, then you probably are going too fast. Slow down. When you can talk about what you've read, then you know you're doing it right.

Don't Look Back   Don't Look Back   Don't Look Back

If you've taken all the steps

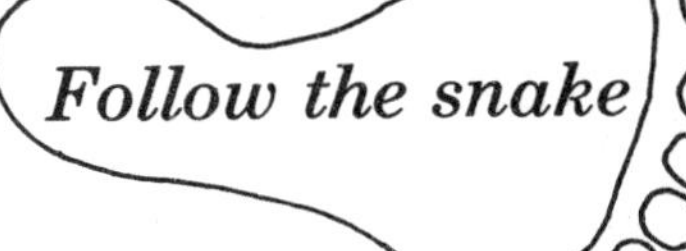

THEN you've earned your Rookie Reader Badge.

SUPER READER SAYS DON'T DO THIS

Don't forget to practice. (It won't work if you don't practice.)

Ben Hogan, a great golfer, used to say, "The more I practice, the luckier I get." Of course, what he meant was that the more he practiced, the better he got.

Don't practice with a book that's too difficult.

**Congratulations!
Here's your
first badge.**

The Reading
Railroad

THE READING RAILROAD

The most serious impediment to effective reading is reading word by word. It slows your child down and actually blocks his comprehension. If a puzzle is divided into eight pieces, it takes more time to put together and to realize what it forms than if it's divided into three pieces. It's like being unable to see the forest for the trees. Your child will soon grasp the concept that words in themselves mean very little— *it is when they are put together that an idea forms.* He should continue using the snake, but now he will read in groups of words or "thought-units," and as he does, his reading speed *and* comprehension will increase steadily.

Begin this chapter by defining your child's development for him. Say, "When you were first learning the alphabet, you were *crawling.* Then, when you were putting the letters and sounds together in order to read, you were in the *walking stage.* Now you know how to read, and you are doing a great deal of reading to yourself. You are beginning the *running stage.* With the help of this book, I am going to show you how to run faster. It may sound a little strange at first, but as you read faster, you will become a much better reader. The way to read for ideas is to read more than one word at a time."

PERIPHERAL VISION

Right now your child may be confused about how she can read three words or more at a time. Begin by telling her that even when she is looking straight ahead, she can see things to the left and to the right. Tell her that the next several pages have exercises to prove it.

Have your child examine the grouping of watermelons and balloons. Show her how to place her finger between the balloons and move it down the page slowly and smoothly, letting her eyes focus lightly above her finger. Then ask, "Did you notice anything unusual as you followed your finger? Did you see the balloons? Did you see the watermelons? Did you notice that you could see all the balloons, and all the watermelons as well?" Explain that she could do this because everyone has something called peripheral vision, p.v. for short. Even when your eyes are focused straight ahead, you can also see things to the left and the right. Tell your child that when she uses her peripheral vision, there is no need to move her head. Let your child practice with the exercises on the following pages until you can see that she is able to use her peripheral vision.

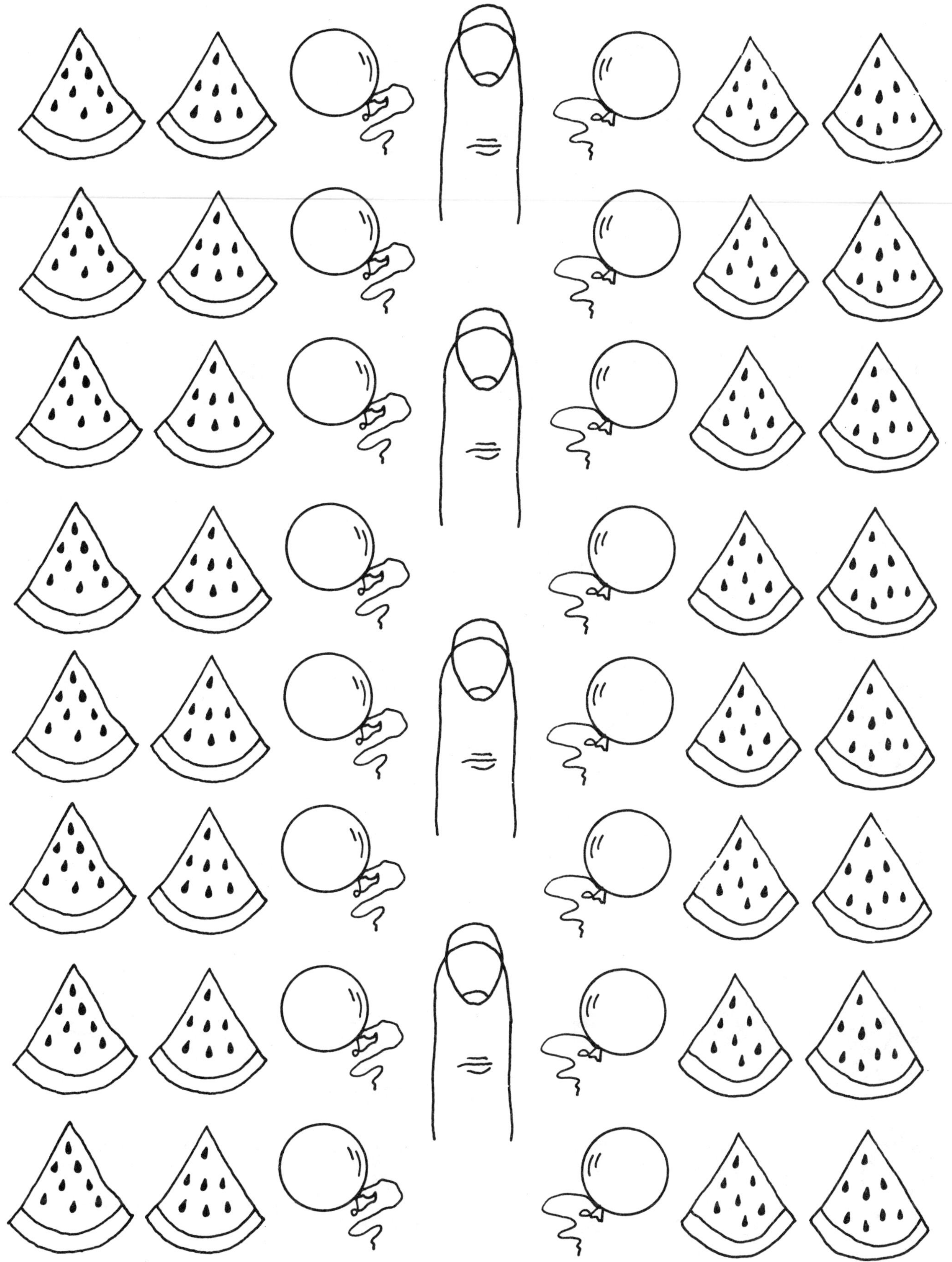

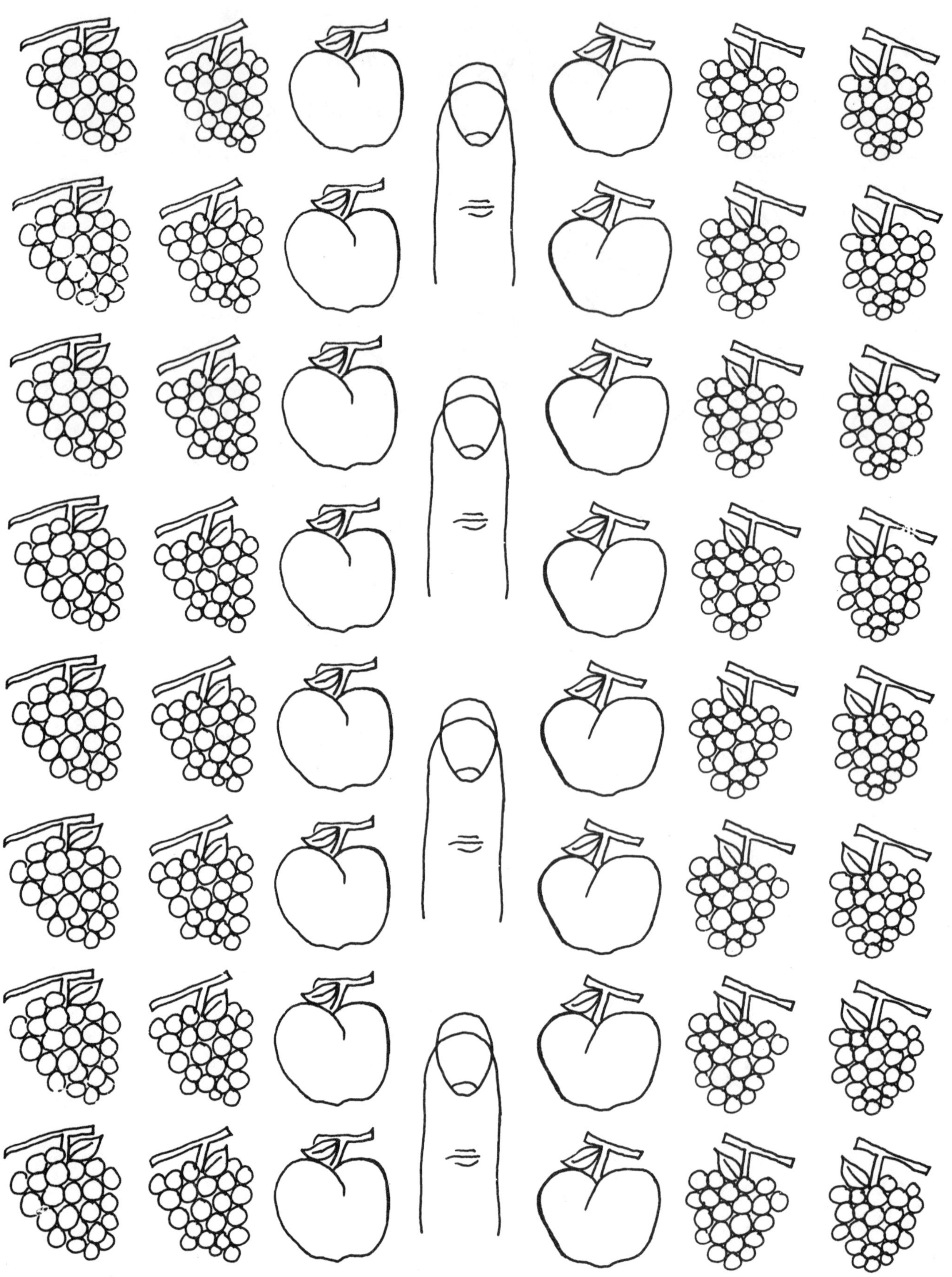

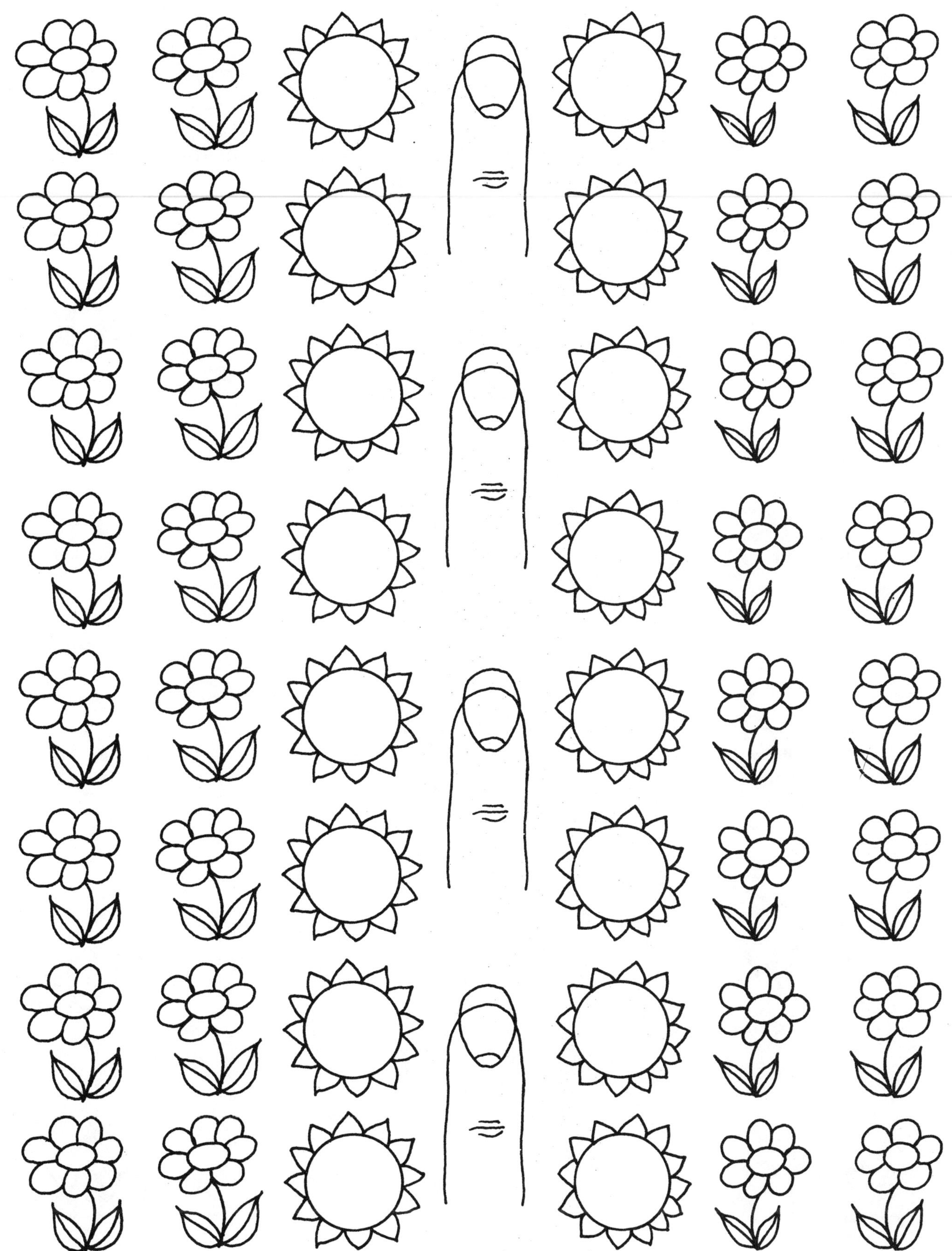

Now let your child do the same exercise with numbers. Ask her if she can see all the numbers while looking above her finger as it slides down the three columns.

108	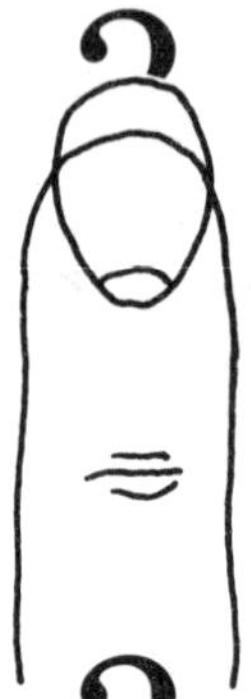	906
108	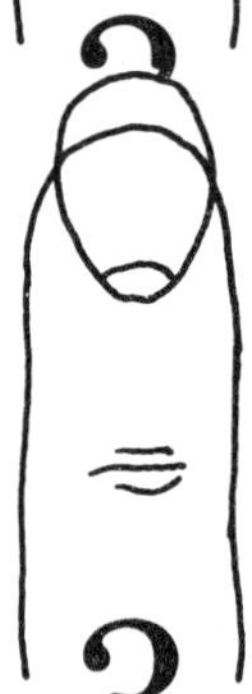	906
108	3	906
108	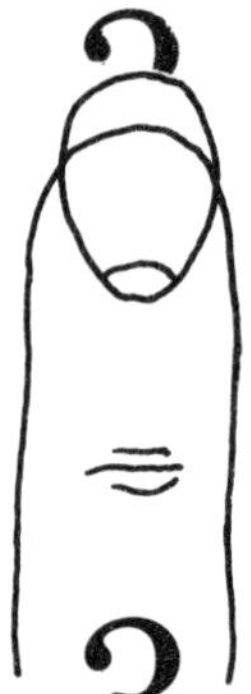	906
108	3	906

Let him use his peripheral vision with letters. (Remind him not to move his head.)

When you see that he has mastered this exercise, celebrate with your child. Tell him how proud you are.

ABC D EFG

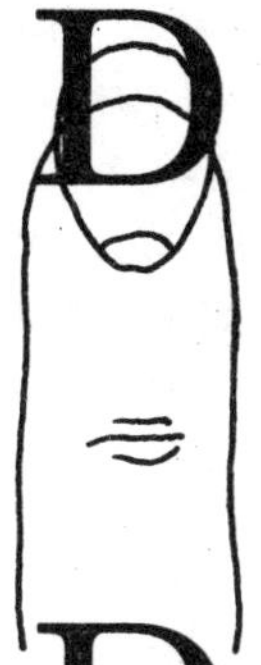

ABC D EFG

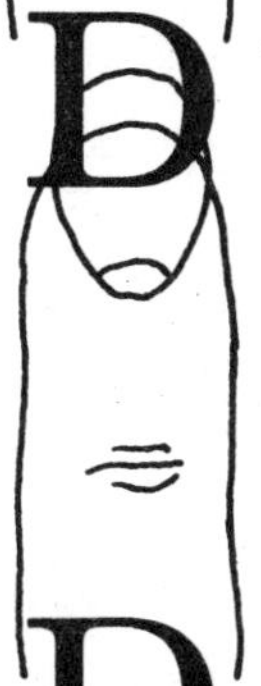

ABC D EFG

ABC D EFG

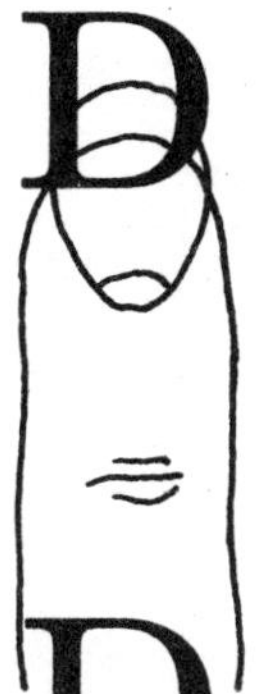

ABC D EFG

THE SPOT

Introduce the next exercise by saying that it is another p.v. exercise, but this time using words that stand next to each other on one line. Explain that the focus of the eye will be the same—above the finger. While the eyes will not move to the left or right, your child should be able to see all the words at once. This is more difficult than the preceding exercise, so go slowly. Explain to your child how the spot has been added to help him center his eyes between two or three words. Instruct your child to place his finger on the SPOT. Ask him if he can see both words while looking at the space between *my* and *house*.

Here is something new—
the spot!

My   house

Remember,
don't turn
your head—
pick up both
words while you are
looking at
the spot.

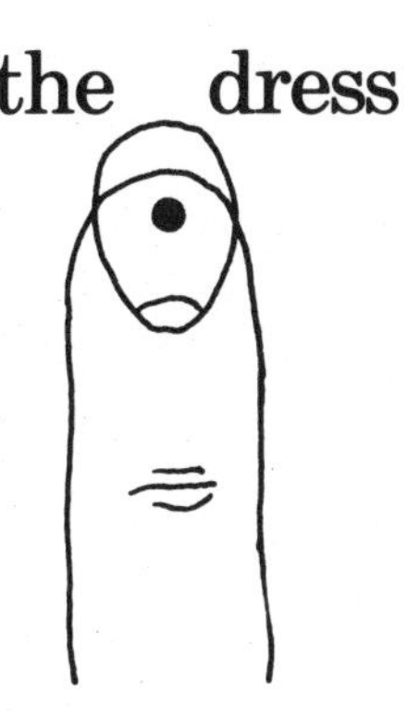

If your child has grasped how to use the spot with two words, you can now go on to three. Instruct your child to place his finger on the spot. Ask him if he can see *in* and *spring* while looking at *the*.

Tell your child not to be impatient. Let him know that his eyes can pick up words that he is not looking at directly. This will be a new discovery for him.

You're doing great!

in the spring

Ask your child if he can see *draw* and *ring* while looking at *a*. If he isn't having any trouble, let him continue the exercises that follow.. If he can't do this, repeat the exercises on the preceding pages.

draw a ring

Reemphasize how it is possible to read more than one word at a time. Show your happiness at his progress by saying, "With one glance you were reading two and three words at a time! How terrific! *This is the key to good reading.*"

The next exercise is the same as the one before except that the words are now in smaller typeface, similar to the type he will be reading in books. Your child should read these phrases *individually. He should pause after each phrase* and lift his finger to get to the next one.

down the stairs

have some breakfast

the main idea

the other day

across the sea

write your answer

ten years ago

in our country

how much money

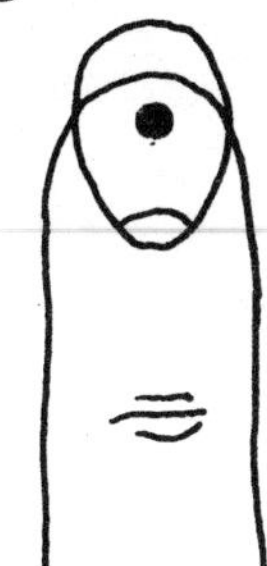

get well

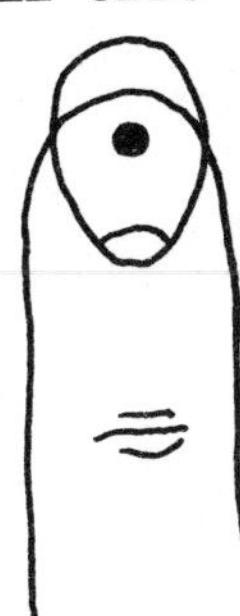

all the time

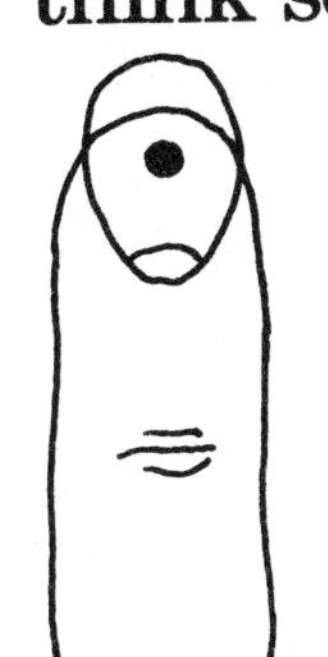

I think so

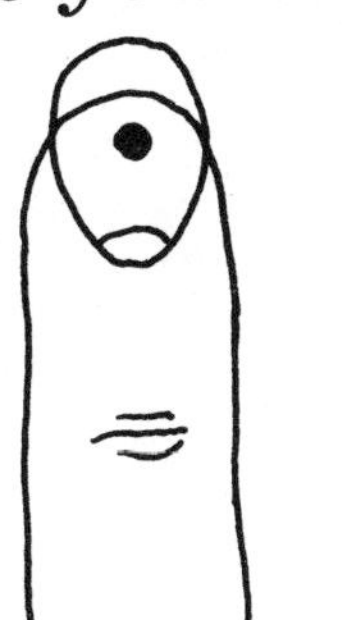

see you later

in the afternoon

on the road

I feel fine

a scraped knee

let him know

Take a Break

after you've read

        stand on your head

                and then to bed

THE READING RAILROAD

Your child has successfully read three words at a glance. We are now ready to prepare him for reading groups of words in sentences.

Explain to your child that we read while our eyes are stopped, not while they are moving. If we read word by word, we make about eight stops for every line on every page of every book we read. As we have learned, p.v. allows us to read many more words than one at a time. We can pick up two and three words per stop and therefore have to make only three stops per line, at most, instead of eight.

Go over the illustration on the opposite page with her. Tell her that the passengers (dashes) stand for words. Explain that the local train operates in a way similar to her old way of reading. At each stop she picks up only one word-passenger and thus has to make eight stops per line to pick up eight passengers. But with her new way of reading, using her p.v., the express train picks up two or three word-passengers at each stop and has to make only three stops to pick up the eight word-passengers.

The Reading Railroad

Eye Local — 1 2 3 4 5 6 7 8

the old way
8 word-passengers—8 stops

Eye Express — 1 2 3

the new way
8 word-passengers—3 stops

Now let your child take a ride on the Eye Express. Show him how to pause (only with his eyes) for a second at the designated spot to pick up two or three word-passengers. Let him take this Eye Express with the word-passengers a few times. In the next two exercises the Eye Express will stop at *words*. The express train (like the snake) doesn't stop; only the eyes do, and they take in a greater number of word-passengers at each glance.

The Eye Express

Your eyes stop (for a second) at the spot as the train chugs along. Follow the train the same way you followed the snake.

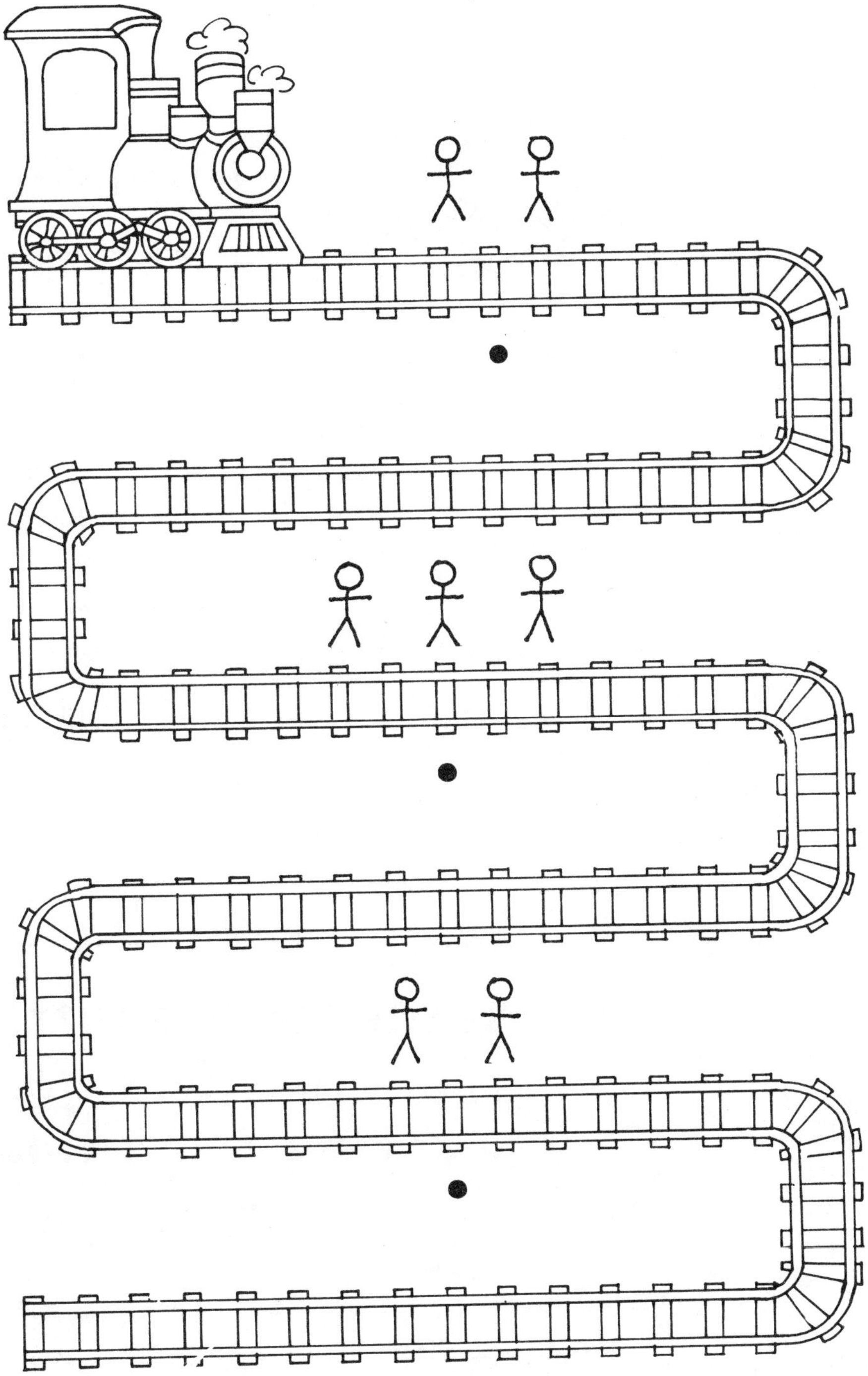

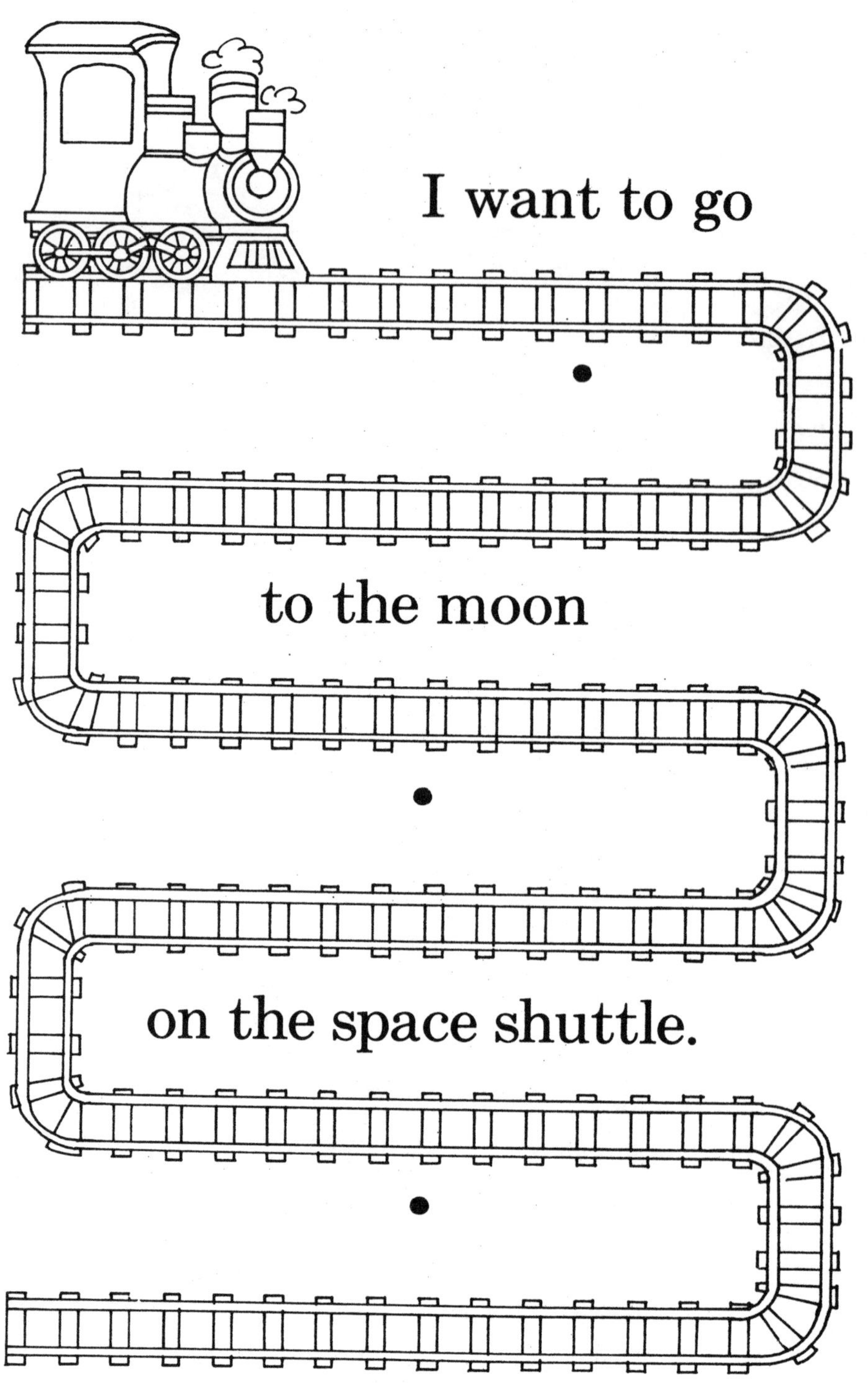

I want to go

to the moon

on the space shuttle.

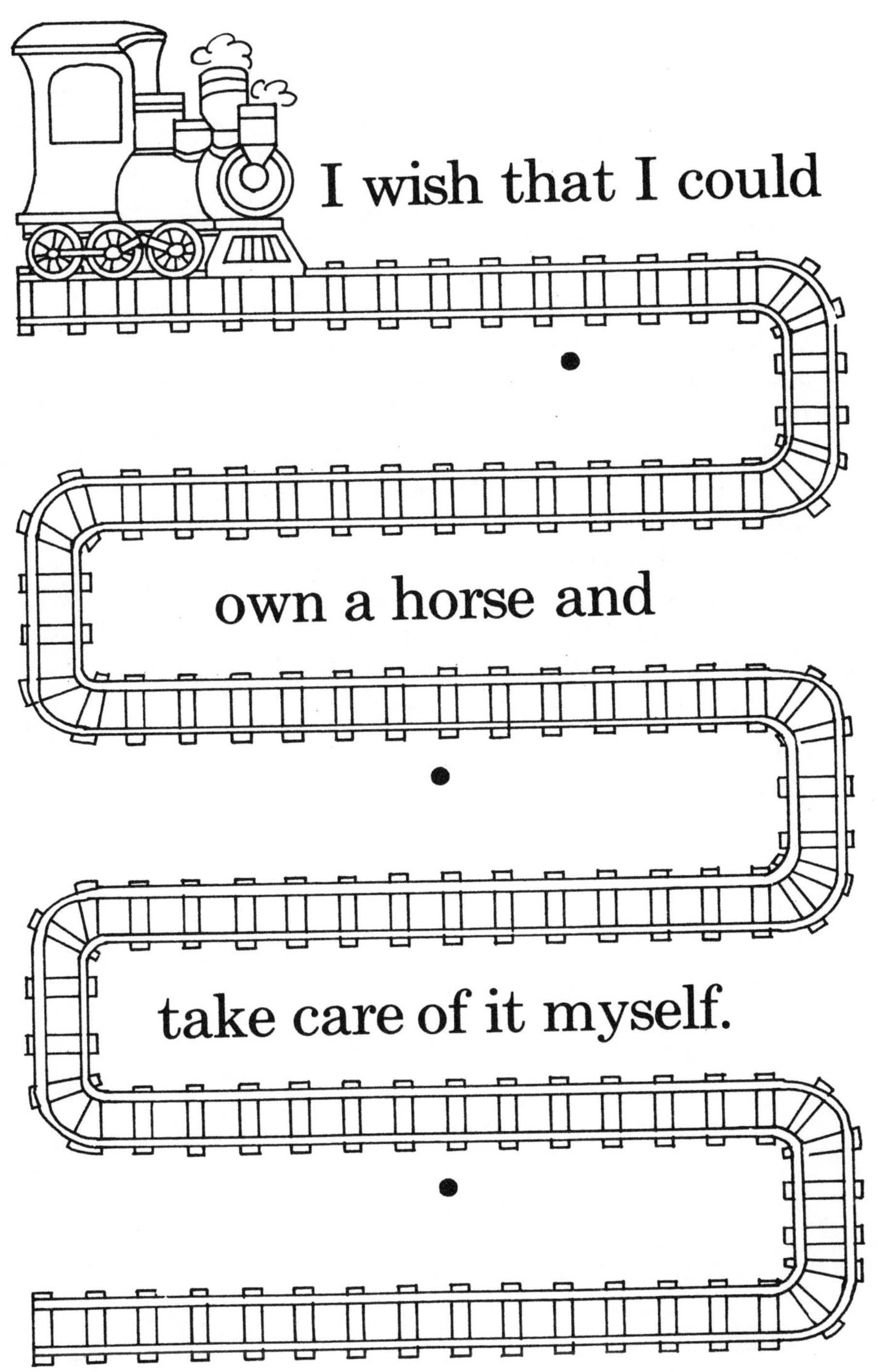

I wish that I could
own a horse and
take care of it myself.

THE SPOTTED SNAKE

Your child is now ready to read groups of words within a sentence. Remind her that she has already read phrases of two and three words using the spot. Add that now that she is experienced in taking the Eye Express, the next exercise should be easy for her. The spot is removed from the train and placed on the snake at the center of groups of words within a sentence. What are we doing? We're starting to streak along with the spotted snake!

When she completes this exercise, ask her how she did. Did she find it difficult or easy? Did she understand what she read? Did she understand that her eyes and mind were working differently than before?

Then tell her how wonderfully she's doing.

Can you follow the
spotted snake?
Remember: don't stop
your finger at
the spot. Keep
your finger following
the snake. Only
your eyes stop at
the spot.

Let's go to the park.

We are having
an important exam
on Monday.

Take a Break

INDENT

Here is a wonderful trick to teach your child. Repeat the explanation about the way p.v. enables you to see to the left and to the right while you are looking straight ahead. Show your child that if he starts reading a line at the first word, he'll be losing his p.v. to the left. In fact, he'll be "reading" the margin. Let him check the example below.

If he begins reading at *We,* half his p.v. will be lost in the left-hand margin. And, if he ends at the word *December,* half his p.v. will be lost in the right-hand margin.

Tell your child the way to utilize all of his p.v. is to INDENT. Begin reading at the second or third word from the margin and stop a word or two before the line ends. Go over the second example with him.

Suggest that your child indent in all his readings. He can practice on the following two paragraphs.

Before

lost | We will be taking our vacation in December. | lost

After

We | will be taking our vacation in | December.

"In a little time I felt something alive moving on my left leg."

From *Gulliver's Travels*
by Jonathan Swift

"But she had met life too bravely to be beaten down now. So,
with a stout heart and a cheery face, she had worked away day after
day at making coats, and tailoring and mending of all descriptions."

From *Five Little Peppers
and How They Grew*
by Margaret Sidney

OUTSIDE READING

Tell your child to continue to practice reading in groups of words with all the easy reading material available where she will be following an *imaginary spotted snake*. Your child should be practicing at least fifteen minutes three times a week. You may coax your child, but do not force her. Make this a pleasant, fulfilling experience for her. Let her be aware that you are enjoying this time with her. Have discussions about the books she's been reading. Do not rush her. This is a skill that requires time to develop.

When it is clear that your child has mastered the skill of following the imaginary spotted snake, celebrate! After she completes the Super Reader Says section, it is time for her to trace, color and pin on her Rapid Reader Badge!

SUPER READER SAYS DO THIS

Practice your P.V. You may want to use the list of phrases I've provided. Why not go over them as often as you like. When they become too familiar, you can ask your mother to make up some more.

Here are some phrases for P.V. Practice

call the doctor	people will know	the party
I invited her	during the summer	after he left
after he fell	of surprises	unable to move
can you go	if I can	summer or winter
how to make	in an hour	through the winter
the old way	go to sleep	next left
at home	mow the lawn	completely wiped out
between jobs	before you go	it's your turn
		I can't go

Take a ride on THE READING RAILROAD a few nights a week.

INDENT   INDENT   INDENT   INDENT   INDENT

Use the DOTTED IMAGINARY SNAKE ON EASY FICTION READING.

If you've taken all the steps

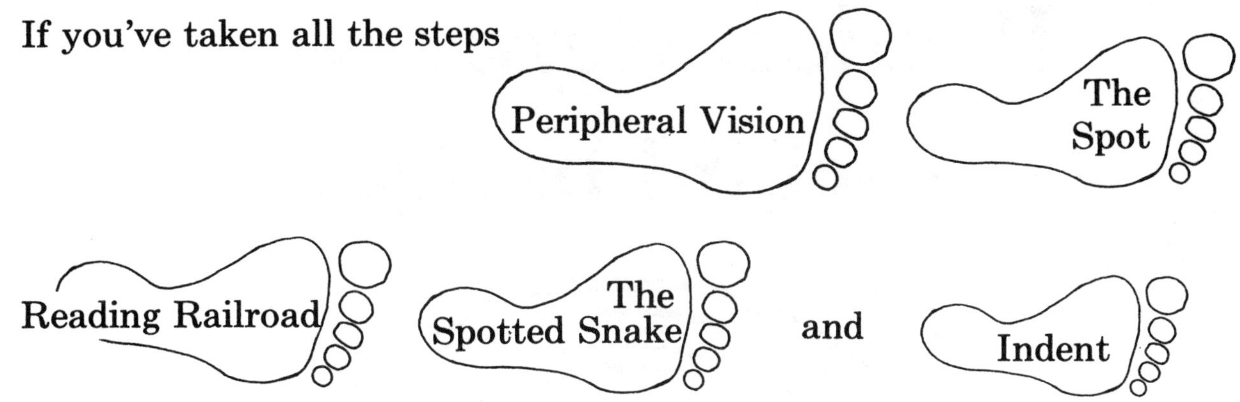

and have continued reviewing these steps

Then you've earned your Rapid Reader Badge.

 SUPER READER SAYS DON'T DO THIS

Don't forget to review the exercises from the last chapter.

Don't be impatient with yourself—learning to Speed Read can't be accomplished overnight.

Don't expect progress without practice.

CONGRATULATIONS! You are now a Rapid Reader. Here's your second badge.

Tulips and Tangerines

TULIPS AND TANGERINES

Ask your child, "Do you believe that you can read numbers or words without saying them either aloud or to yourself?" If he seems confused by the question, ask him to read a page from one of his favorite books. Then ask him if he knows whether he said the words to himself as he read—either by mouthing the words, or by moving his vocal cords, or by merely "saying" the words in his mind. He will probably say yes. This habit can be very difficult to break, but with practice, your child can learn to become less and less dependent on it. When you read the old way, you can read only as fast as you talk. But an experienced reader is a "sight" reader. He sees the words, and the message goes from the eyes directly to the brain, without first forming in the mouth. It is a difficult transition to make because your child was taught to say each sound to make words as he was first taught how to read. A sight reader bypasses the vocal and auditory reflexes. If the child's eyes are forced to *read faster* and take in *groups of words,* it will be much more difficult to "say" the words.

OVERCOMING VOCALIZATION

Vocalization occurs when a child makes sounds in her throat or moves her lips as she reads to herself.

To prevent your child from making sounds in her throat, let her try to *blow out air* through a straw as she reads. It sounds silly, but it works.

To eliminate the habit of moving her lips as she reads, *give your child a straw or pencil to hold in her lips.* If the pencil moves about or falls to the floor, she will know that she's lip-reading.

Another way to break this habit is to have your child *chew gum* while she reads.

Here is a selection to practice on. Have your child *continue practicing on other paragraphs from her favorite books until the habit is broken.*

Also check on comprehension by asking your child to do a *Read and Recite* with a reading selection of his own choice.

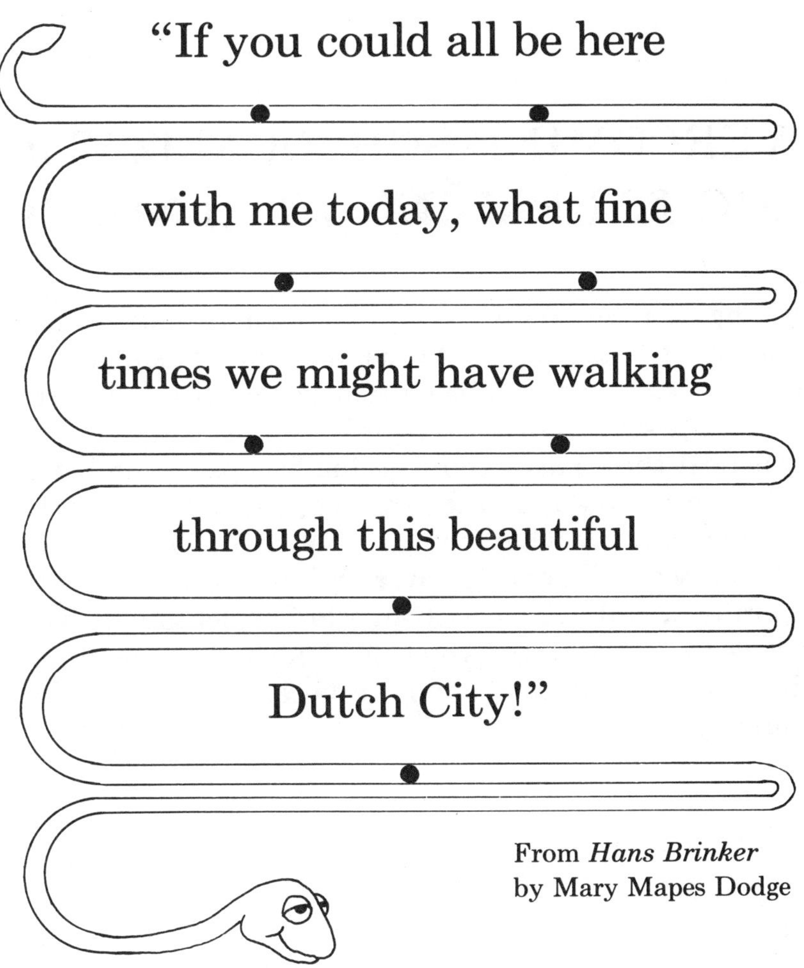

From *Hans Brinker*
by Mary Mapes Dodge

Hold a pencil
between your lips.
Don't let it drop.

Now try chewing gum
(sugarless) while you
read the selection again.

OVERCOMING SUBVOCALIZATION
BY SIGHT-READING WITH NUMBERS

The following exercises are designed to overcome your child's subvocalization, the habit of saying the words in his mind as he reads. The first group of exercises is based on the premise that if you are reading very fast, you can't possibly "say" the words as you read.

On the next three pages you will find groups of numbers. Cover the first number with a blank index card and instruct your child to glance at the numbers quickly when you uncover them. Uncover the numbers for less than a second. Then re-cover and immediately ask the child to say the number aloud. If he has them all right, let him continue. Cover-uncover-cover again. Remind your child not to say the numbers in his mind. He probably will not be able to because you are covering them over so quickly.

Can you sight read?

102   435

24   78

630   590

402   347

14   58

420   798

1190   3465

2121   1938

425   167

537   400

415	788
711	5842
25	1007
1306	6559
14	2749
477	156
524	234
608	1102
892	405
406	518

46	21
58	356
20	422
31	105
89	786
531	1032
415	534
44	908
15	2346
1050	6227

OVERCOMING SUBVOCALIZATION BY SIGHT-READING WITH FUNNY WORDS

Now tell your child that she is going to do the same exercises, but this time with words. Cover each word grouping. Uncover the words for less than a second. Then cover them again and have your child say the words aloud.

After she's read a few of the phrases, ask her, "Now do you believe that you can read words without saying them in your mind? Of course you do. You've already done it. *You were sight-reading!*"

How did your child do? If she had any difficulty, remember to be patient and helpful. Repeat the exercise until she can see all the words. Never pressure your child. If she has trouble with the exercise, drop it and return another day. Keep the atmosphere cheerful.

Merry Christmas

Happy New Year

Let's go home

Play ball

Muffin and me

Go home now

We won

Summer in the city

All the way

Hit the ball

Hello again

Here we go

Time out

School is over

Love and kisses

To the top

Eat your lunch

See you later

Exercise today

Time out

Black and blue

His and hers

Ready or not

You are my sunshine

To the moon

Little League

Apples and oranges

Sing and dance

Read a book

The Super Bowl

Take a Break

At this time
May I suggest
That you give
Your brain a rest?

OVERCOMING SUBVOCALIZATION BY SIGHT-READING WITH WORDS

The next group of exercises will utilize what we have learned in the preceding chapters. In the exercises that follow, the "snake finger" will pace the eyes, taking in groups of words at a glance. But now your child will have *something else to say aloud*—other words—to keep him from "saying" the words he's reading in his mind.

The funny words are on the opposite page. For the exercises that follow, have your child choose one word or phrase to repeat aloud as he reads. If he gets tired of one phrase, try another—or make up one of your own.

NOTE: This is an extremely difficult exercise. If your child can do it, that's wonderful. If he can't, don't pressure him. This step is not essential to "sight" reading. It is something extra.

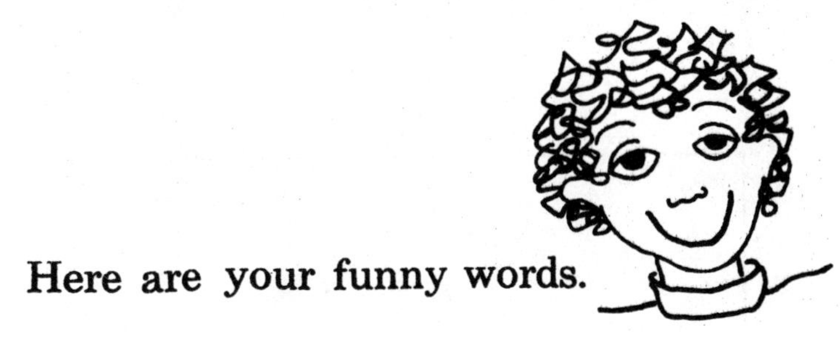

Here are your funny words.

Tulips

Tangerines

Kangaroo

Scarecrow

Monsters

or

ABC   123   buzz

la de da   Okay

or

your name

or any other word or sound

FINGER MITTENS

So that your child will have more fun pacing while she is overcoming subvocalization, you might like to make her a set of finger mittens. You can make finger mittens by tracing, cutting out, and then coloring the figures on the opposite page. Cut off the fingers of a pair of old gloves and paste on the cutouts. Then choose a funny phrase or word and match the finger mitten to it.

Let's begin the exercise with the *Tulip.* Have your child put on the tulip finger mitten. Tell him to *repeat the word* tulip *over and over again aloud* as he reads the selection. Have him read the selection ten times.

At first he probably won't understand what he's read. That's okay. Insist that he continue to practice, and his comprehension will improve gradually.

When you are pacing to "Kangaroo,"
wear this.

Here is the finger face for
"Monsters."

And the finger face
for "Tulips."

And "Scarecrow."

"Tangerines."

From "Rumpelstiltskin," *Grimm's Fairy Tales*

Now say Tangerines over and over again aloud as you read this selection.

From *The Three Musketeers*
by Alexandre Dumas

From *The Adventures of Tom Sawyer*
by Mark Twain

Try Kangaroo.
How did you do?

How about
Scarecrow!
Remember to
read in groups
of words as
you follow
the snake.

Now it's a
Monster's turn.
Monster, Monster, Monster.

From *A Tale of Two Cities*
by Charles Dickens

From *The Wind in the Willows*
by Kenneth Grahame

Take a Break

I interrupt
this book to say,
It's time to put
this book away.
(For awhile.)

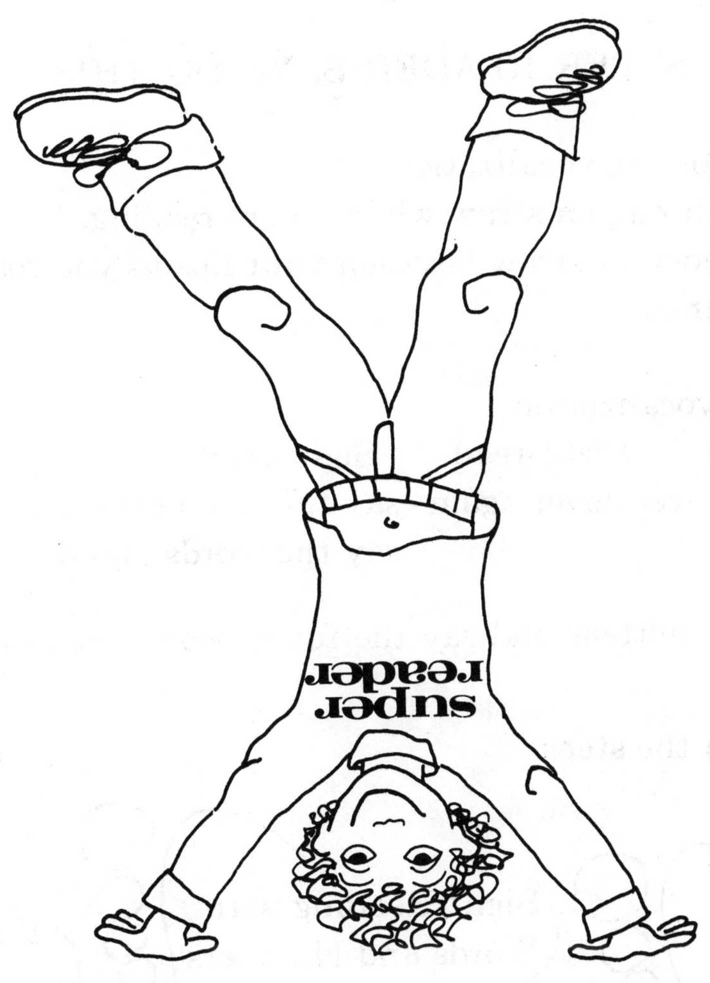

OUTSIDE READING

Let your child continue practicing with easy fiction. At first he will have difficulty understanding what he's reading because he has been so dependent on his audio-vocal reflexes. But gradually he will become a "sight" reader. Do not rush him. It may take a matter of several months. Let him go at his own pace.

When your child seems to have achieved confidence as a "sight" reader and has completed the Super Reader section, give him his Accelerator Reader Badge.

SUPER READER SAYS DO THIS

Practice overcoming vocalization

    Blow air through a straw while you're reading.

    Place a pencil or straw between your lips as you read and chew gum (sugarless).

Overcome subvocalization

    Sight-read   Sight-read   Sight-read

    Cover-uncover-cover again—say the numbers aloud
                             say the words aloud

Wear the finger mittens and say the funny words aloud as you read.

If you've taken the steps

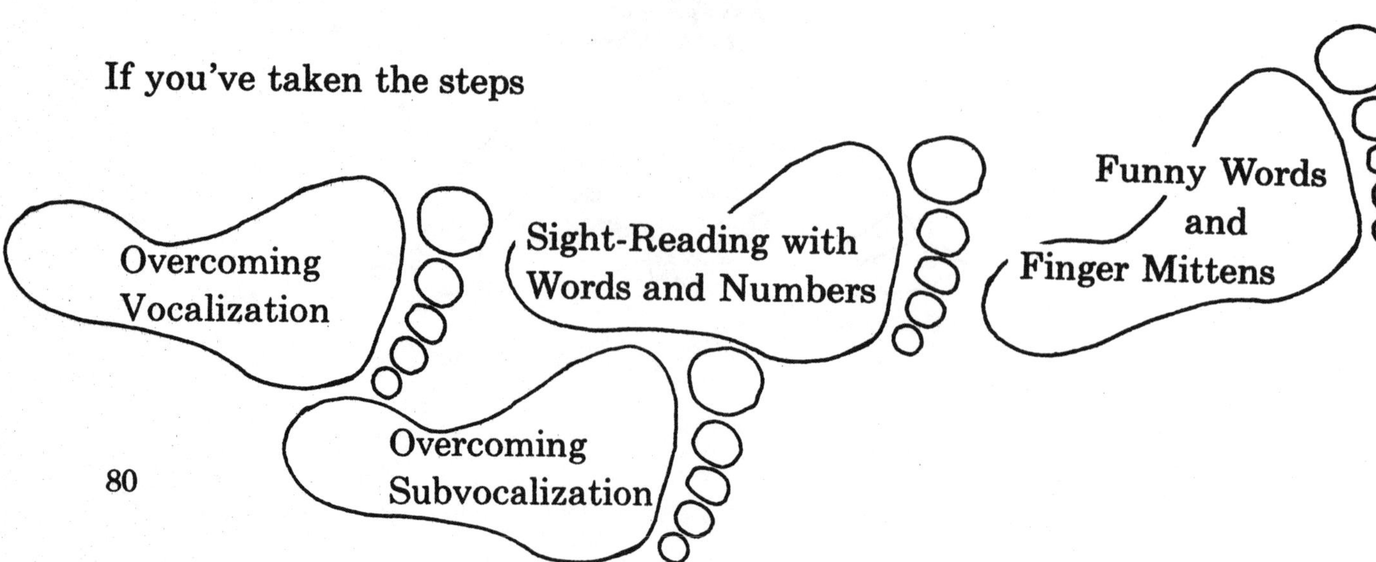

and continue to review

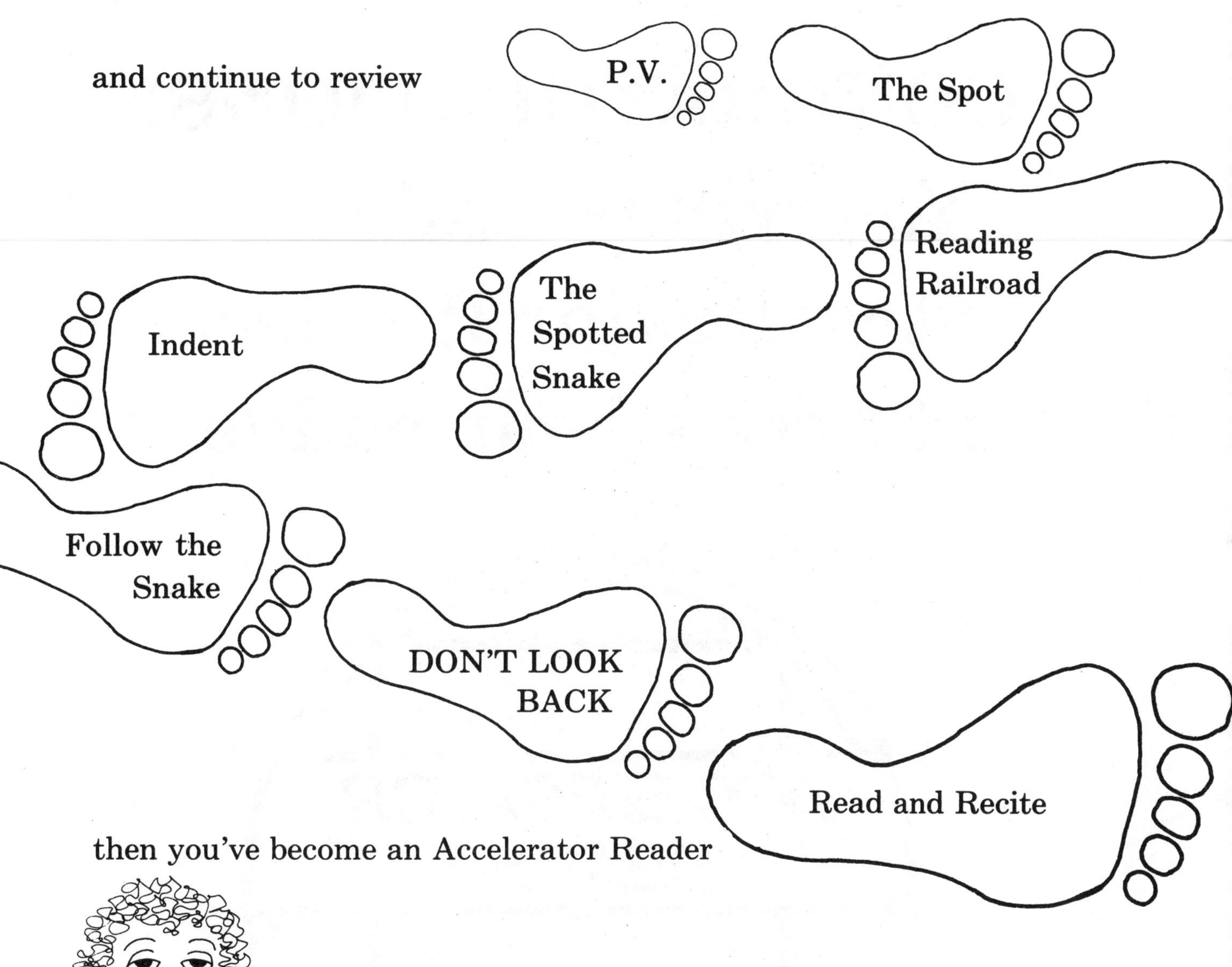

then you've become an Accelerator Reader

SUPER READER SAYS DON'T DO THIS

1. Don't forget to have your mother, father, or teacher make up new sight-reading phrases for you when the list becomes too familiar.

2. Don't rush yourself with the funny phrases and finger mittens. It is an extremely difficult exercise, and the slightest improvement is fantastic.

3. Don't forget to stick to a schedule.

CONGRATULATIONS!
You will be called an Accelerator Reader. And here's your badge.

The Super Reader Olympics

THE SUPER READER OLYMPICS

Your child is now ready for the Super Reader Olympics. She has been practicing for months to prove herself worthy of the title Super Reader, and the Gold Medal that goes with it. Much time has been spent on following the snake. Reading in groups of words has become second nature. Vocalization has disappeared, and your child is less dependent on the habit of subvocalization. Tell your child that the kangaroos, monsters, tulips, and scarecrows are all standing by and rooting for her. They're rooting for her speed and her comprehension. Let's see what she can do at the Olympics.

QUALIFYING WARM-UPS

Introduce the Qualifying Warm-ups. Your child should thoroughly review each step he has taken in order to qualify for the Super Reader Olympics. After your child reads the name of a step, he should explain what it means and show how to do it. If he has difficulties with any step, go back and practice it with him.

When he completes all ten steps, then he has passed the Qualifying Warm-ups and can move on to the hurdle-jumping competition.

Qualifying Warm-ups

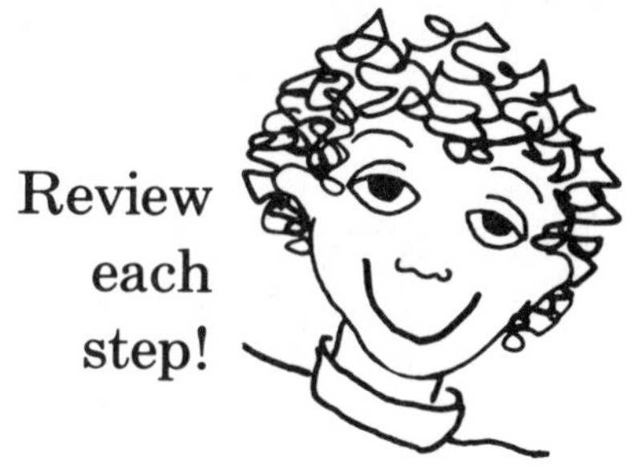

Review
each
step!

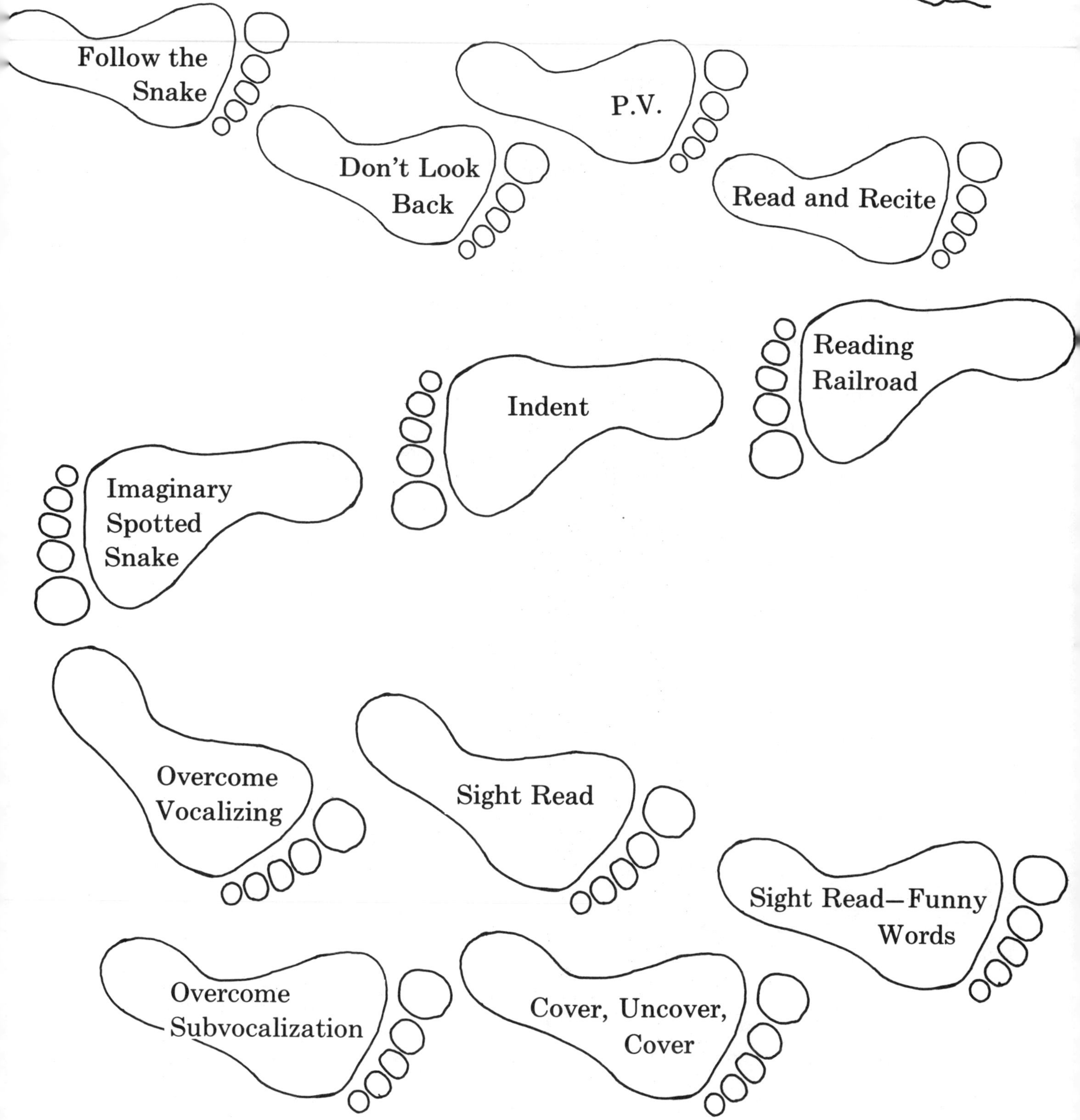
Follow the Snake
P.V.
Don't Look Back
Read and Recite
Reading Railroad
Indent
Imaginary Spotted Snake
Overcome Vocalizing
Sight Read
Sight Read—Funny Words
Overcome Subvocalization
Cover, Uncover, Cover

JUMP THE HURDLES AND
READ, REMEMBER, AND PATTERN

Now that your child has completed the Qualifying Warm-ups, she is ready to jump the hurdles. The hurdles are *read, remember,* and *pattern.* Tell your child that the *read, remember,* and *pattern* combine to form a method which will enable her to improve her reading comprehension and retention by writing down the highlights of what she's just read. Teach her how to do this by saying, "After reading a selection, add everything up in your mind; the thoughts, the images. Keep some things, lose others. Compare, interpret, and wind up with a center, a core, a main idea. Take this core and give it a shape, a visual form drawn on the page. It will be a lot clearer than the usual outline or summary. That's really what it is—a basic outline that's been all jazzed up." Tell your child to either use the shapes suggested in the text or make up her own. Remind her that the shapes will show the most important ideas of the reading selection and their relationship to each other. Go over the "The Hare and the Tortoise" example with her. Let her *read* the selection, *remember* the highlights and their relationships, and then see how the read-and-remember *pattern* was made.

The Hare and the Tortoise

A hare was continually poking fun at a tortoise because of the slowness of his pace. The tortoise tried not to be annoyed by the jeers of the hare, but one day in the presence of the other animals, he was goaded into challenging the hare to a foot race.

"Why, this is a joke," said the hare. "You know that I can run circles around you."

"Enough of your boasting," said the tortoise. "Let's get on with the race."

So the course was set by the animals, and the fox was chosen as judge. He gave a sharp bark and the race was on. Almost before you could say "scat," the hare was out of sight. The tortoise plodded along at his usual unhurried pace.

After a time the hare stopped to wait for the tortoise to come along. He waited for a long, long time until he began to get sleepy. "I'll just take a quick nap here in this soft grass, and then in the cool of the day I'll finish the race." So he lay down and closed his eyes.

Meanwhile, the tortoise plodded on. He passed the sleeping hare and was approaching the finish line when the hare awoke with a start. It was too late to save the race. Much ashamed, he crept away while the animals at the finish line acclaimed the winner.

A Read-and-Remember Pattern
The Hare and the Tortoise

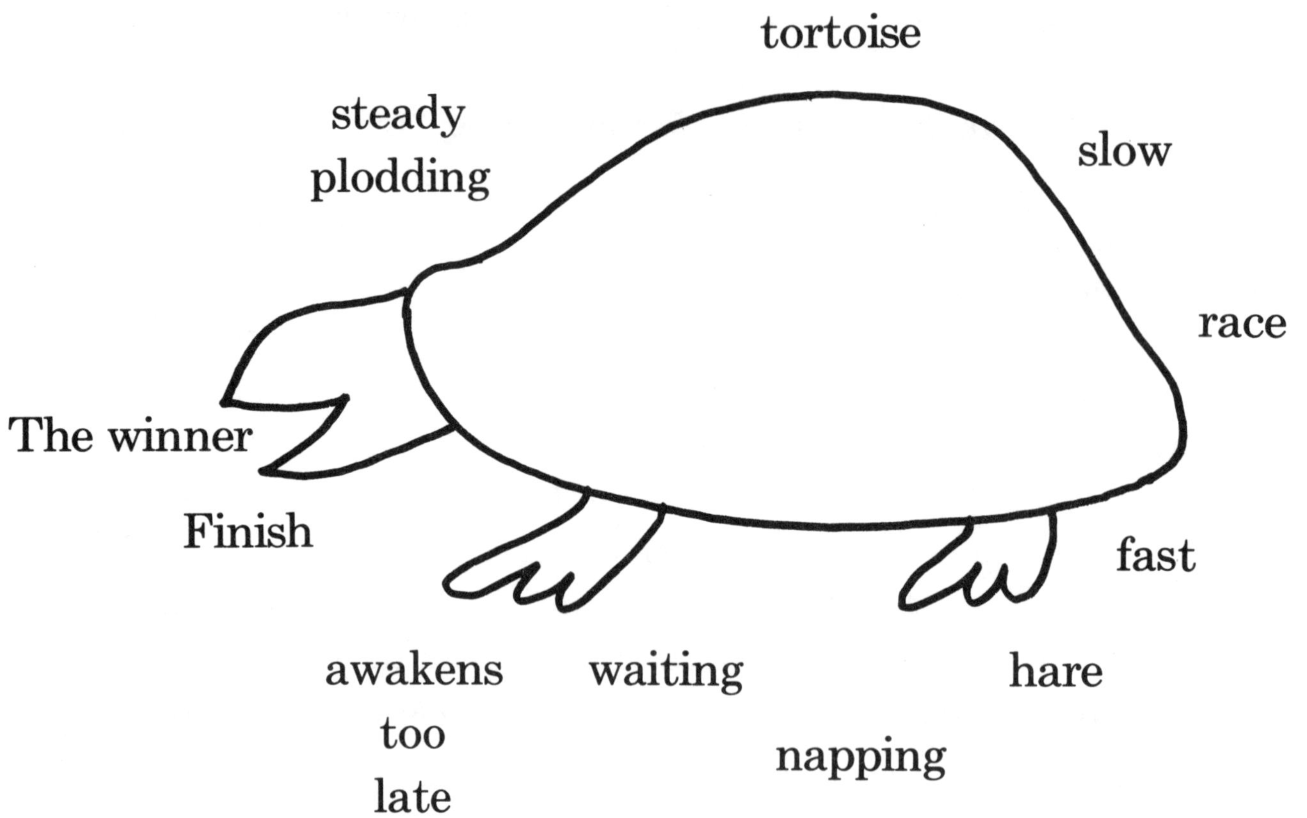

Can you see how
the two main
characters and
their actions are
made into a pattern?

Read-and-Remember Patterns

Here are four shapes you can use for a read-and-remember pattern. Or you can make up some of your own.

Branch

Robot

Sunshine

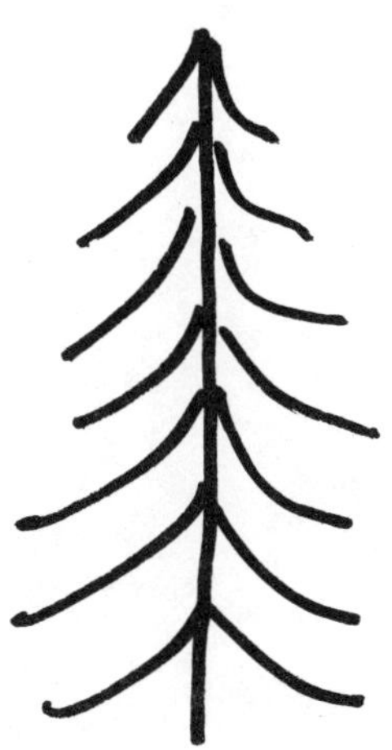

Christmas

JUMP THE HURDLES

Now let's see if your child can jump the hurdles. For his first hurdle, instruct him to *read* the next selection. Then he should *remember* the highlights and their relationship to each other. If he can do that, he will have jumped the second hurdle. The third hurdle requires him to make a read-and-remember *pattern*. He can use one of the patterns already shown or make up one of his own. After he has jumped all three hurdles, he is ready to run the laps. But first suggest that he should try to make read-and-remember patterns in his own outside reading from now on.

Jump the Hurdles

See if
you can
jump
the
three
hurdles.

READ

"Mr. Fox was just about famished, and thirsty too, when he stole into a vineyard where the sun-ripened grapes were hanging up on a trellis in a tempting show, but too high for him to reach. He took a run and a jump, snapping at the nearest bunch, but missed. Again and again he jumped, only to miss the luscious prize. At last, worn out with his efforts, he retreated, muttering: 'Well I never really wanted those grapes anyway. I am sure they are sour and perhaps wormy in the bargain.' "

Moral: Any fool can despise what he cannot get.

From "The Fox Grapes," *Aesop's Fables*

REMEMBER

PATTERN

Take a piece
of paper and
do your own
pattern for
this selection.

RUN THE LAPS, AND DATE AND RATE

Your child is now ready to start running the laps.

THE FIRST LAP: READ AND TIME

Before your child begins to read, let her mark her beginning spot. Tell her to read for one timed minute, using a cooking timer. Let her see how much she can read before the bell goes off. Instruct her to mark her ending spot.

THE SECOND LAP: DATE AND RATE

Here are the instructions for rating. Make sure your child understands how to do this. After she finishes reading the selection:

1. Write the date for your records.
2. Count the number of words in the first line. Let's say there are eight words.
3. Count the number of lines read. Let's say she's read 20 lines.
4. Now multiply the number of lines read by the number of words on each line

$$\begin{array}{r} 20 \\ \times 8 \\ \hline 160 \end{array}$$

The result is a Reading Rate of 160 words per minute.

Suggest that your child continue to time herself every so often as a means of testing her skills. If she maintains a certain rate or increases her reading rate, she should be aware of it. Praise her. If her rate decreases, then perhaps she hasn't been practicing enough. Maybe she needs more encouragement.

Have your child continue running the laps a few nights a week. He will be able to keep a record of his progress on the Date and Rate chart. See if he's improving. Praise him if he is. If he isn't improving, don't let him get discouraged. If there are times when his rates go down, it might mean that what he read was too difficult or that he worked or played too hard before he started reading.

Run the Laps

Lap 1   Read and Time

       and

Lap 2   Date and Rate

Here's how you rate yourself:

Write the date________________________
Write the number of words
in the first line______________________
Write the number of lines read__________
Then multiply the number of lines by the
number of words on each line __________
Reading Rate_________WPM.__________

There's a sample chart on the next page.

DATE AND RATE CHART

Here's an example of a Date and Rate chart.
Now try to make your own.

Date	and		Rate
May 2	Number of lines read	20	180 wpm
	Number of words per line	x9	
		180	
May 6	Number of lines read	20	210 wpm
	Number of words per line	x10	
		210	

 You mustn't stop using your new skills.
If you do, you will surely lose them.

Follow the Snake

Don't Look Back

Read and Recite

P.V.

Reading Railroad

Indent

Spotted Snake

Overcome Vocalization

Overcome Subvocalization

Sight-read
(cover uncover cover)

Sight-read
(funny words)

Warm-ups

Qualifying

Run the Laps

Jump the Hurdles

If you've passed the Qualifying Warm-ups, and continue to Jump the Hurdles and Run the Laps, you have reached the top, and you are now privileged to be called a SUPER READER!

The Word Collector

THE WORD COLLECTOR

If your child can increase his vocabulary, he will certainly become a better reader. In order to make words live for your child, first talk to him about words. You can say you and he are now entering Word-world, a world of words—big words, little words, fat words, skinny words, funny words, serious words, sad words, new words, and old words.

What are words? Words are communications, signals, connections, impressions we give to other people and to ourselves. Words help to illuminate our experiences. If we know more words, our world expands. It becomes more colorful and more interesting. Words are the connecting threads that weave themselves through the fabric of our lives. We need words to give, to share, to express, to learn. This chapter offers many ideas, games, and exercises to help your child discover new words.

Teach your child to become a word collector. To begin, try something like this: "Becoming a word collector is better than being a collector of other things, because even though stones are precious and stamps are intriguing and butterflies are gorgeous, you can't carry them around with you all the time and use them. But if you become a collector of words—a *Word Collector*—you always have them with you and you can use them all the time. They will never lose their value or fade or wear out. Words are tireless, healthy, and steadfast."

Then continue with a new theme: "Collecting words is good for you, too! All the hints and fun-filled games and interesting exercises in this section are fine, but *you have to love words*. They must live for you, or none of the exercises will work. It's all up to you."

You can suggest that your child begin word collecting by writing any new words which she finds interesting on slips of paper or index cards. Have her write the meaning of the word and a sentence using the word. She might enjoy keeping these in a drawer. (See if she can fill it up.)

Wall Words

List 10 of your favorite words and then explain why each one is a favorite of yours. After you've done this, ask your child to do the same, using some of the words he has collected and put on his file cards. Then compare the words and discuss them. Because of what these words as symbols represent to you, you will have experienced memories, unusual feelings, and funny imaginings.

Ask your child what topics interest him the most. Then, find 10 words related to that topic and write them with a red crayon in large letters on stiff paper to be hung all over your child's room. (You may wish to do the same in your room.) The definitions will be behind the word. These will stay up for one week, and then another topic will be chosen. Continue for as long as you can sustain interest. If his interest lags, discontinue for a week or two. Then begin again. You may wish to use synonyms for Walls Words. There are nine lists on page 100.

Wall Words

Here are
two sample
wall words

mare	female horse
ballot	method of secret voting

Politics
ballot
campaign
caucus
convention
dark horse
incumbent
opposition
plurality
nominee
debate

Horses
bridle
girth
stall
lope
canter
mare
colt
prance
thoroughbred
quarter horse

Travel
compass
departure
log
itinerary
reservation
souvenir
terminal
venture
voyage
route

happy
content
joyous
glad
cheerful
serene
harmonious
pleased
exhilarated
elated
optimistic

sad
unhappy
gloomy
discontent
unfortunate
melancholy
dismal
miserable
wretched
pessimistic
somber

pretty
attractive
comely
good-looking
cute
lovely
handsome
graceful
fine
charming
picturesque

extraordinary
unusual
singular
uncommon
remarkable
phenomenal
abnormal
rare
notable
eminent
great

walk
saunter
scamper
shamble
scurry
strut
clamber
tread
totter
stroll
swagger

awkward
clumsy
ungraceful
embarrassing
bungling
unskillful
inexperienced
inept
incompetent
ungainly
gauche

All words are pegs to hang ideas on.

Henry Ward Beecher
Proverbs from Plymouth Pulpit (1887)

A word is dead
When it is said, some say,
I say it just
Begins to live
That day

*Selected Poems and Letters of
Emily Dickinson* (1872)

Words form the thread on which we string our
experiences.

Aldous Huxley,
The Olive Tree (1937)

The difference between the right word and the
almost right word is the difference between lightning
and the lightning bug.

Mark Twain

IT'S ALL THE SAME TO ME

Next you can introduce the *Synonym Time Game*. Explain to your child that the game can be played by two or more people. Each person writes five words on separate slips of paper. The slips are then placed in a box or a bowl. One person at a time takes out a word, says the word, and the other person, who has become the timer, gives him one minute to name or write down as many synonyms as he can.

After the first player's time is up and his answers are checked, the turn passes to the next player. Continue until there are no slips of paper left. Now count the number of synonyms each player has. The player with the greatest number wins. (When a disagreement arises, use a dictionary to check the answers. You may also want to purchase a thesaurus.)

You can begin by playing the first few games with your child. Afterward, if there are no brothers, sisters, or friends for him to play with, you can show him how to play alone. Tell him simply to choose a word, time himself, and see how many synonyms he can list in a minute. Explain to him that he is challenging himself. Encourage him to continue trying to increase the number of synonyms for each word. For example, let's say that when he began he could name only three or four synonyms for each word. Tell him that probably after a few weeks of playing this game he should be able to name seven or eight synonyms for each word. This is because he has become more conscious of words with similar meanings.

It's All the Same to Me

ALL ABOUT AN AVERAGE APPLE

Introduce the second alphabet game, *All About an Average Apple,* by explaining that two or more people can play together or one person can play alone. The game begins with letter A. A cooking timer is used. The child is given one minute to name as many words as she can that begin with A. Then B, C, D, and all the way to Z.

When your child is playing with someone else, each child has a minute to list as many words as he can. They are then added up, and whoever has the most words wins. If your child is playing alone, have her keep a record and suggest that she continue trying to increase the number of words she lists for each letter. Let her try doing a letter a day, and when she finishes the alphabet, let her begin again.

Remind your child that she can play this game walking to school, waiting on the lunch line, or while riding in the car with the family.

All About an Average Apple

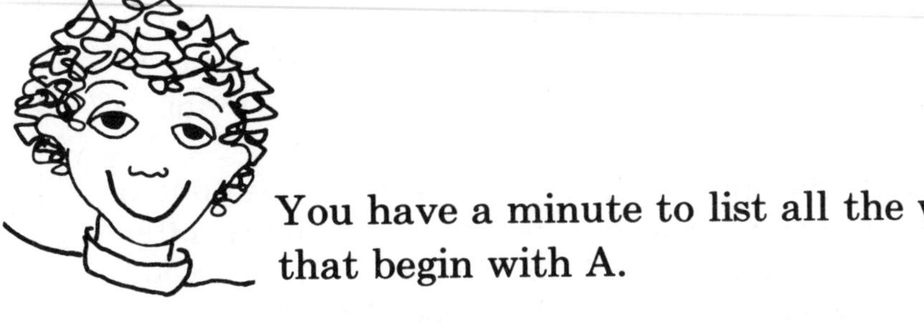

You have a minute to list all the words you can that begin with A.

A ——————

   ——————

   ——————

   ——————

   ——————

   ——————

   ——————

   ——————

   ——————

Then B, C, D, and all the way to Z.

A YOU'RE ADORABLE B YOU'RE SO BONY

It's not Monopoly, but I think your child will enjoy it anyhow. Explain that the first part of this alphabet game entails going through the alphabet saying to a friend or relative: A you're adorable, B you're so bony, C you're ______, D you're too ______, E you're ______, F you're ______, etc.

See if you can go all the way to Z. After your child has done it once, he can always do it again because it becomes very funny, often hilarious. Children's imaginations run wild in this game. Try it yourself. Or you can take turns with your child. You take A, then he takes B and so on.

Have fun!

A You're Adorable . . .

Try this.

A you're adorable   B you're so bony

C you're ________________

D you're too ________________

E you're ________________

F you're _______________

G you're so _______________

H you're too _________ I you're _________ J you're too ___________

K _______________

L _______________

M _______________

N _________

O _______________

P _______________

Q _______________

R _______________

S _______________

T _______________

U _______________

V _______________

W _______________

X _______________

Y _______________

Z _______________

Opposites Attract

big   little
            small
            tiny

small   huge
            large
            enormous

pretty

____

____

____

____

fast

____

____

____

____

sad

____

____

____

____

love

____

____

____

____

CRIMSON IS A COLOR

The principle of one-minute timing with two or more players (or with one child alone) is the same for this game. You and your child will choose a category, for example, flowers, trees, birds, colors, animals, foods, fish. Then see how many names each of you can list under the main category.

Here are three examples:

Flowers	**Birds**	**Trees**
Orchid	Robin	Willow
Forget-me-not	Song sparrow	Banyan
Daffodil	Wren	Cedar
Geranium	Bluebird	Eucalyptus
Violet	Hummingbird	Maple
Carnation	Oriole	Redwood
Tulip	Cardinal	Hickory
Hyacinth	Chickadee	Cypress
Rose	Eagle	Elm

Now you're on your own! Take a blank piece of paper and make a separate column for colors, horses, or fish, or anything else you want to list.

Colors	**Horses**	**Fish**
______	______	______
______	______	______
______	______	______
______	______	______

Remind your child that all the games and exercises in this section can be used over and over again. You may decide to buy your child word-game and crossword-puzzle books to provide additional stimulus.

If your children have completed all the word games, plan to continue learning new words, and have a drawer at least half full of words, then they've earned the Word Collector Badge.

Cheers!

You have now completed all the word games, and you plan to continue learning new words, and have a drawer at least half full of words. You have earned the Word Collector Badge.

Congratulations!

The Super Reader Song

Music and Lyrics copyright © 1978 by Jonathan L. Segal